A CULTURAL HISTORY OF WOMEN IN AMERICA

The Modern Feminist Movement: Sisters Under the Skin 1961–1979

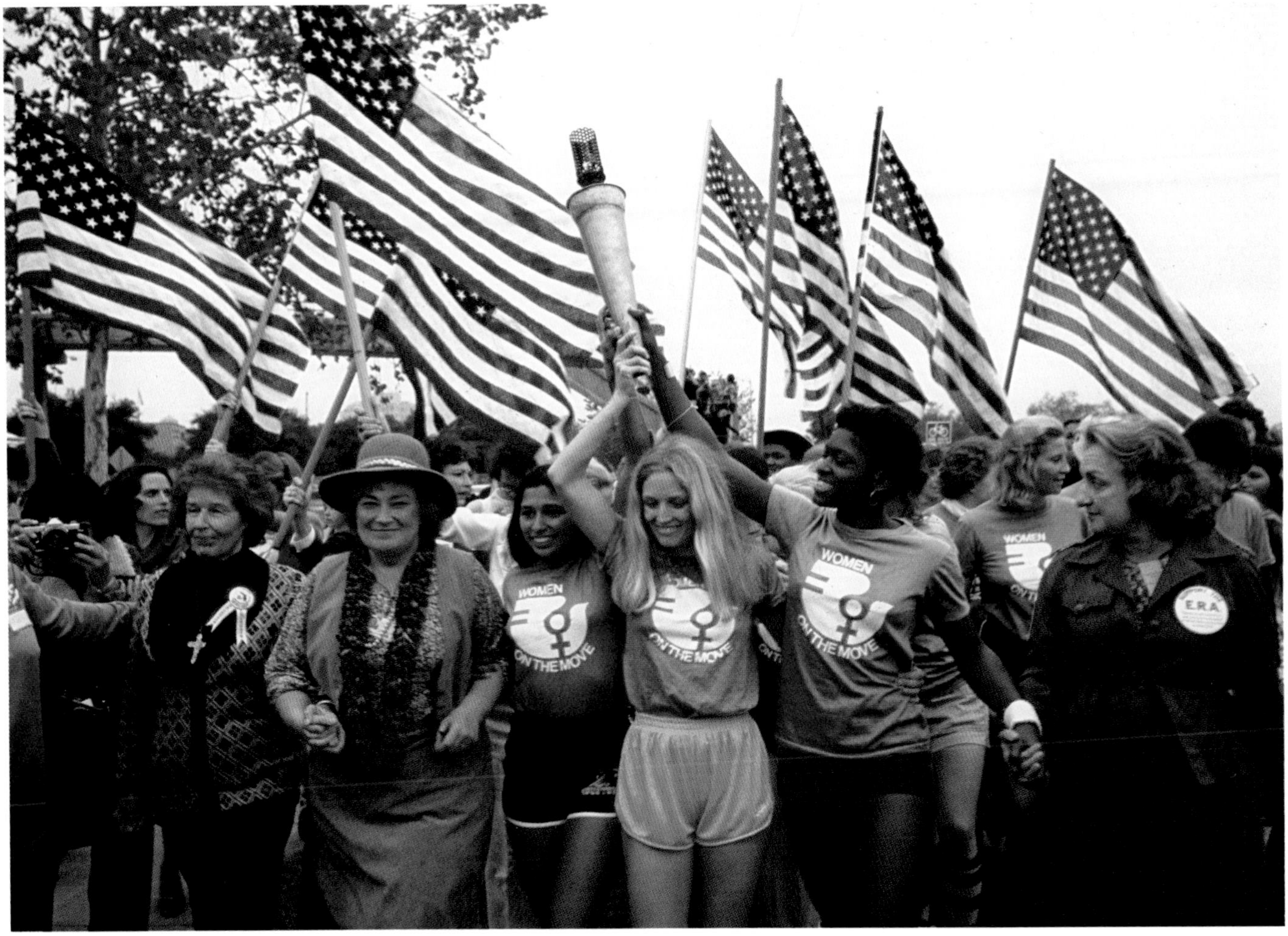

JACQUELINE LAKS GORMAN

CHELSEA HOUSE
An Infobase Learning Company

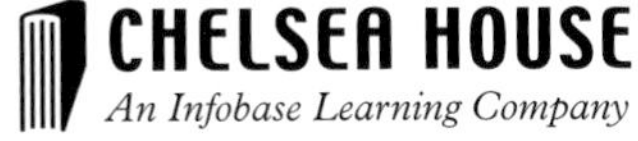

THE MODERN FEMINIST MOVEMENT: SISTERS UNDER THE SKIN 1961–1979

Produced for Chelsea House by Bailey Publishing Associates Ltd, 11a Woodlands, Hove BN3 6TJ, England

Library of Congress Cataloging-in-Publication Data

Gorman, Jacqueline Laks, 1955–
The modern feminist movement : sisters under the skin, 1961-1979 / Jacqueline Laks Gorman.
p. cm. — (A cultural history of women in America)
Includes index.
ISBN 978-1-60413-935-8
1. Women—United States—Social conditions—20th century—Juvenile literature. 2. Feminism—United States—History—20th century—Juvenile literature. 3. Women's rights—United States—History—20th century—Juvenile literature. 4. United States—Social conditions—1960–1980—Juvenile literature. I. Title. II. Series.
HQ1421.G67 2011
305.420973'09046—dc22

2010045990

Chelsea House books are available at special discounts when purchased in bulk quantities for businesses, associations, institutions, or sales promotions. Please call our Special Sales Department in New York at (212) 967-8800 or (800) 322-8755.

You can find Chelsea House on the World Wide Web at http://www.chelseahouse.com

Project management by Patience Coster
Text design by Jane Hawkins
Picture research by Shelley Noronha
Printed and bound in Malaysia
Bound book date: April 2011

10 9 8 7 6 5 4 3 2 1

This book is printed on acid-free paper.

All links and Web addresses were checked and verified to be correct at the time of publication. Because of the dynamic nature of the Web, some addresses and links may have changed since publication and may no longer be valid.

The publishers would like to thank the following for permission to reproduce their pictures:
Corbis: 5 (Bettmann), 6 (H. Armstrong Roberts/ClassicStock), 8 (Bettmann), 9 (Farrell Grehan), 10 (Bettmann), 11 (Bettmann), 19 (H. Armstrong Roberts/ClassicStock), 22 (Bettmann), 23 (Bettmann), 24 (Roger Ressmeyer), 25 (Michael Ochs Archives), 29 (Bettmann), 30 (JP Laffont/Sygma), 31 (Bettmann), 32 (Bettmann), 33, 34 (David J. & Janice L. Frent Collection), 35 (Bettmann), 37 (Dean Conger), 39 (Bettmann), 42 (Vince Streano), 43 (Condé Nast Archive), 47 (Shepard Sherbell), 48 (Roger Ressmeyer), 49 (Bettmann), 53 (Bettmann), 54 (Michael Ochs Archives), 56 (Lynn Goldsmith), 57 (Pollock-Krasner Foundation/Artists Rights Society (ARS), New York); Getty Images: 12 (Time & Life Pictures), 15, 21 (Time & Life Pictures), 38 (Time & Life Pictures), 46 (Time & Life Pictures), 51; The Kobal Collection: 50 (CBS); Rex Features: 27 (CSU Archv/Everett), 28 (CSU Archv/Everett), 36 (Everett), 59 (NBCUPHOTOBANK); TopFoto: 7, 14 (The Image Works), 16 (The Image Works), 17 (The Granger Collection), 18 (ClassicStock), 20 (AP), 26 (The Image Works), 40 (The Image Works), 41, 44 (The Image Works), 45 (The Image Works), 52 (AP), 55 (The Image Works), 58 (The Granger Collection); Topham Picturepoint: 13.

Contents

The 1960s and 1970s were a time of significant change in the United States. During these years, people began to challenge widespread ideas about the place of different groups in society. Activists in the civil rights movement fought against segregation and struggled for equality for African Americans. Newly politicized students on college campuses rose up to confront authority and young people embraced a counterculture of innovative music, clothing, and attitudes. People of all ages organized and took to the streets—sometimes violently—to protest involvement of the United States in the war in Vietnam.

Women were one of the groups of people who demanded change. Frustrated and dissatisfied with the limits placed on them, women joined together to discuss what they wanted from their lives, to work for equal rights, and to demand a full place in American society. Modern feminism and the women's rights movement began in the 1960s, and the resulting changes became part of life in the 1970s.

The 1960s was the beginning of the "second wave" of feminism. The first wave took place in the 1800s, when suffragists fought for the right to vote in addition to other rights for women. The first-wave feminists won some of their goals—most notably, the vote—but there was still much to be achieved during the second wave of feminism in the 1960s and 1970s.

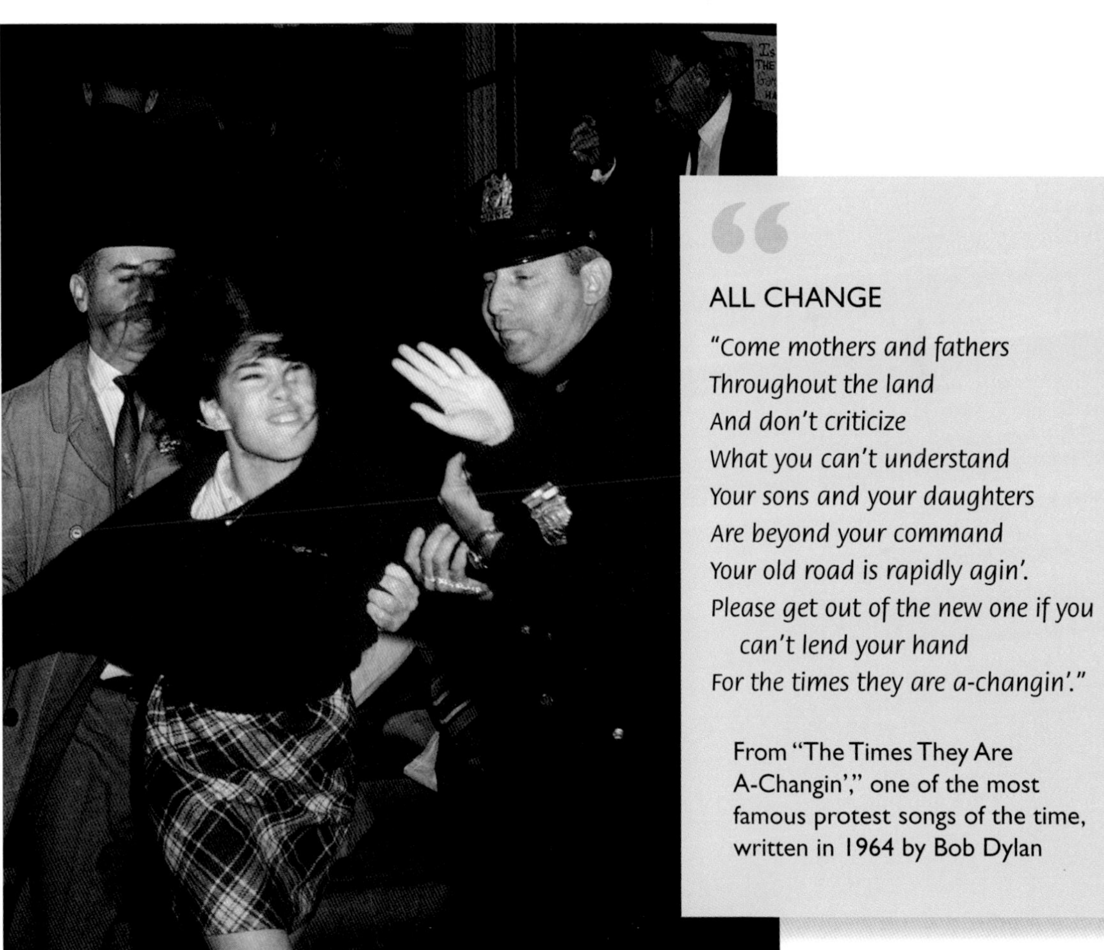

Right: During a 1967 antiwar protest at Brooklyn College in New York City, a student struggles with police after her arrest. The 1960s and 1970s were a time of change and protest in the United States.

ALL CHANGE

"Come mothers and fathers
Throughout the land
And don't criticize
What you can't understand
Your sons and your daughters
Are beyond your command
Your old road is rapidly agin'.
Please get out of the new one if you can't lend your hand
For the times they are a-changin'."

From "The Times They Are A-Changin'," one of the most famous protest songs of the time, written in 1964 by Bob Dylan

CHAPTER 1

An Unequal World

A young woman growing up in the early 1960s did not have many choices about what her life would be like. Her place in society was not equal to a man's, even though she most likely was not aware of the extent of the limits placed on her. Many of her rights or opportunities were different from a man's, and she was not expected to do the same things. Her life was restricted because of society's rules, traditions, and views.

EXPECTATIONS AND LIMITATIONS

A woman in the early 1960s was expected to get married, stay home, and have children, and it was assumed she would be content with this role. For her, success was seen as having a husband with a good job who could provide for his wife and family. Few people thought a woman might have or even want a fulfilling occupation outside the home. If she did have a job when she was younger, she was expected to stop working once she got married and certainly after she had children.

In the early 1960s, those women who worked generally had low-paid jobs in factories or the service industries. The vast majority of working women were employed in jobs such as secretaries, waitresses, and beauticians. Women tended to be teachers but not principals, nurses but not doctors, and typists but not business executives.

Left: Women in the early 1960s were expected to be happy homemakers. This woman—preparing lunches for her children to take to school—appears happy from the photograph.

Above: Few women in the 1960s were in positions of authority. Here, a female secretary and her male boss look over a document.

TWO'S COMPANY?

"Yes, indeed, we do take women, and we do not want the one woman we take to be lonesome, so we take two per class."

A spokesman for a medical school in the early 1960s, giving his reasons for the institution's admissions policy regarding female students

LOW PAY

Women were also paid much less than men. The typical female bank teller, for example, earned $15 a week less than her male counterpart. On average, a woman working full time earned only 60 cents for every dollar earned by a man.

If a woman sought a better job, she discovered that many occupations—especially those involving greater power and higher pay—were simply not open to females. Only a small number of women made it to the top professions. In 1960 women made up only 6 percent of the doctors in the United States, 3.5 percent of the lawyers, and less than 1 percent of the engineers. Women constituted only 10 percent of the nation's scientists and less than 2 percent of top business executives.

WOMEN NEED NOT APPLY

Few women held positions at any levels of government. In 1960, there were only two women in the U.S. Senate out of a total of one

WOMEN OF COURAGE AND CONVICTION

JANET MCCLOUD (1924–2003)

Janet McCloud was a Native American woman born on the Tulalip Reservation in Washington State. She helped launch the Native American rights movement of the 1960s and 1970s. In the early 1960s, McCloud and other women staged a series of "fish-ins" in Washington. They were protesting government efforts to restrict the rights of Native people to fish freely—rights that had been granted in old treaties. After their husbands were arrested for breaking state laws by fishing for salmon, the women took their places in the boats and were arrested too. The fish-ins continued for years, with McCloud among the most visible activists. Finally, in 1974, a federal district judge ruled in favor of the Native American groups. Later, McCloud traveled widely to spread her message of women's rights and social justice for all.

hundred senators. There were only seventeen women in the House of Representatives out of a total of 435. Of 7,700 state legislators, only 234 were female; there were no women justices on the Supreme Court, no women governors, none serving in the president's cabinet, and no women ambassadors.

The message delivered to women and girls through schools, the legal system, and popular culture was clear—they were not supposed to compete with men and boys. They were not expected to be independent or think for themselves. Their fathers and later their husbands would make all the decisions and control most aspects of their lives.

BEING LADYLIKE

Television programs and popular magazines of the time often portrayed women as foolish, jealous of one another, and irresponsible with money. Women were also shown as being greatly concerned about their appearance—and many were. No matter what they were doing, they almost always wore makeup. Unless she was employed in a factory, the

TURNING POINT

CAMELOT AT THE WHITE HOUSE

When John F. Kennedy became president of the United States in 1961, he and his wife, Jacqueline, ushered in a new era in national politics. They were young, glamorous, and cultured, and the Kennedy White House was hailed as Camelot—a reference to the court of the legendary King Arthur. All things seemed promising and possible for the nation. Jackie in particular enchanted women with her stylish clothes, elegance, and graceful air. Women wanted to dress like her, style their hair like her, and be like her. During the 1960 presidential campaign, Kennedy's advisers had suggested that Jackie stay in the background because she was so different from the average American. She was, for example, from a wealthy background, had gone to private schools, went foxhunting, and had an air of formality. The public loved her, however, and she was one of the most popular first ladies. Public admiration for her grew even stronger after John Kennedy was assassinated in November 1963. The image of the brave young widow, left to care for two small children, touched Americans' hearts.

Right: Jacqueline Kennedy—shown with her husband, President John Kennedy—brought culture and elegance to the White House in the early 1960s.

average woman in the early 1960s wore a dress and nylon stockings at work. She also generally wore a dress when she did housework and even when the weather was cold. Pants were acceptable only in very casual situations.

Since most women did not participate in sports or athletic activities, wearing dresses may have seemed appropriate. Indeed, young women had few opportunities to compete in high school or college sports. Women were also discouraged from participating in certain sports because the activity might be too strenuous or "unladylike." It was even thought that some sports might damage a woman's ability to bear children. There were certainly no girls allowed to play Little League!

TURNING POINT

THE MINISKIRT

In 1965, British designer Mary Quant launched the miniskirt. At first only young, daring women wore the extremely short skirts, which could be as much as 8 inches (20 centimeters) above the knee. Miniskirts were worn with pantyhose, which also became popular in the 1960s and replaced stockings held up by awkward and uncomfortable girdles or garter belts with clips. Miniskirts stood for youthful rebellion, liberation, and freedom. They became less popular in the late 1960s when many girls turned to the "hippie" look, characterized by jeans with bell bottoms, long peasant dresses, tie-dyed shirts, beads, flowers, and Indian prints.

Below: In the early 1960s, high-school girls seldom participated in sports. Instead, they could be cheerleaders, like these teenagers from Hempstead, New York.

CHAPTER 2

Modern Feminism Begins

THE 1960S WAS A DECADE OF TURBULENCE AND UNREST. Throughout the United States, tensions that had been growing for years erupted, and people joined together to protest unfairness, discrimination, and social situations they felt were unacceptable. Different social movements—such as the civil rights, antiwar, and student protest movements—took shape and came alive. The modern women's movement began as well.

THE SECOND WAVE

Women who were active in the civil rights, antiwar, and student movements came to realize that their own situation was not acceptable either. The first-wave feminists had worked both for women's rights and the abolition of slavery. In much the same way, socially active women in the 1960s helped launch a new wave of feminism to work for their own equality.

Below: President John Kennedy (center, seated) after signing the Equal Pay Act of 1963, to ensure that employers gave women the same pay as men for doing the same work.

THE PRESIDENT'S COMMISSION

One development that helped to spur the modern feminist movement occurred at the government level. President Kennedy had no women in his cabinet. Esther Peterson, the head of the Women's Bureau in the Department of Labor, was the highest-ranking woman in his administration. A longtime labor activist, Peterson was interested in ensuring that women received equal pay for doing the same work as men. She suggested that Kennedy create a group to investigate the condition of women in the United States.

In 1961, the President's Commission on the Status of Women was created, made up of eleven men and thirteen women, including Peterson. It was led by Eleanor Roosevelt, a former first lady known for her interest in social justice who died in November 1962, before the commission had completed its research. The commission's report was issued in 1963 on her birthday—October 11.

The report found widespread discrimination against women in practically every area of American life, including employment and the law. It called for continued efforts by the government to ensure equal rights for women and to clarify (make clear) women's legal status under the U.S. Constitution. A number of specific recommendations were made, including setting up child-care centers for working mothers and continuing education and

THE SILENT QUESTION

"The problem lay buried, unspoken, for many years in the minds of American women. It was a strange stirring, a sense of dissatisfaction, a yearning that women suffered. . . . Each suburban wife struggled with it alone. As she made the beds, shopped for groceries, . . . ate peanut butter sandwiches with her children, chauffeured Cub Scouts and Brownies, lay beside her husband at night, she was afraid to ask even of herself the silent question: 'Is this all?'"

Betty Friedan, in *The Feminine Mystique* (1963)

WOMEN OF COURAGE AND CONVICTION

FANNIE LOU HAMER (1917–77)

Fannie Lou Hamer was the granddaughter of slaves and the youngest of twenty children of Mississippi sharecroppers. In 1964 she led a group of African Americans, called the Mississippi Freedom Democratic Party, to the Democratic National Convention. They were protesting Mississippi's all-white delegation to the convention. Hamer delivered a dramatic speech that was televised to a national audience. She talked about losing her job, being beaten, and going to prison for her efforts to help African Americans register to vote. "I'm sick and tired of being sick and tired," she said. The Democratic Party leadership pledged that in 1968, all delegations to the convention had to include African-American representatives.

Left: Fannie Lou Hamer helped many African Americans register to vote.

BREAKTHROUGH BIOGRAPHY

BETTY FRIEDAN (1921–2006)

Betty Friedan was born in Peoria, Illinois. She graduated from Smith College in 1942. She then studied psychology in graduate school at the University of California at Berkeley and became a writer. In 1947, she married and later had three children (she divorced in 1969). After writing *The Feminine Mystique*, Friedan became a leader in the fight for women's rights. In 1966, she became the first president of the National Organization for Women (NOW), and later helped found such groups as the National Association for the Repeal of Abortion Laws and the National Women's Political Caucus. Friedan was a controversial figure, however, sometimes criticized for seeming to focus on white, educated, middle-class women rather than recognizing the issues of minority and lower-class women.

Above: Betty Friedan (at right, in red coat), is shown here taking part in a 1977 women's march. Friedan played an important part in launching the modern feminist movement with her 1963 book *The Feminine Mystique*.

vocational training programs for women. The commission also called for ending restrictions on the rights of married women, withdrawing bans on women serving on juries during trials, promoting more women to high-level government jobs, and appointing more women to policy-making positions.

State and local governments appointed their own commissions to look into the status of women and propose changes that should be made. Within a few years, all of these efforts—especially on the national level—led to laws on giving women equal pay and opportunities. The laws did not always succeed, however, and were hard to enforce. There was still much to be done to ensure equality for women.

A NAMELESS PROBLEM

While government commissions were meeting and reporting on women's roles in such areas as work and politics, many women were thinking about more personal matters. In large part, this was because of *The Feminine Mystique*, a book written by Betty Friedan in 1963. Friedan had sent questionnaires to two hundred of her classmates from

Smith College (an all-women's school) to mark their fifteenth reunion in 1957. She discovered that many of the women were not happy, despite being financially comfortable and having husbands, children, and nice homes. Friedan questioned other women and wrote articles about her findings. The results of her research were published as *The Feminine Mystique*, in which she stated that educated, middle-class women in America were suffering from "a nameless, aching dissatisfaction" with their lives. She called it "the problem that has no name."

The Feminine Mystique became a bestseller. Women read it and realized they were not alone in their discontent—others felt the same way that they did. Perhaps, they thought, it was all right—even understandable—for them to want something more than a husband, a house, and a family. In many ways, *The Feminine Mystique* sparked the modern feminist movement. Women who read it realized that things could change—they could go back to school, go to work, and demand an equal place in society.

WOMEN OF COURAGE AND CONVICTION

KATE MILLETT (1934–)

Katherine Murray Millett was born in St. Paul, Minnesota. She graduated from the University of Minnesota when she was just seventeen years old and then studied literature at Oxford University in England. She taught English at Barnard College but was fired because she participated in a student strike at Columbia University in 1968. Millett had become interested in feminism, and in 1970, her controversial book *Sexual Politics* was published and became a bestseller. In it she discussed the many male writers who had created negative images of women. Millett published several other books but also experienced personal problems. She was criticized for her radical views and made national headlines when she revealed that she was a lesbian. She was also diagnosed with bipolar disorder and institutionalized for a time. In recent years, Millett has run a Christmas tree farm and women's art colony in New York State.

Below: Writer Kate Millett's book *Sexual Politics*, published in 1970, was one of the first works of modern feminist theory.

DEVELOPING POTENTIAL

"We believe the time has come . . . to confront, with concrete action, the conditions that now prevent women from enjoying the equality of opportunity and freedom of choice which is their right, as individual Americans, and as human beings. NOW is dedicated to the proposition that women, first and foremost, are human beings, who, like all other people in our society, must have the chance to develop their fullest human potential."

From NOW's "Statement of Purpose," 1966

PROTESTING SECOND-CLASS STATUS

Women played an active role in the social movements of the 1960s. Both African-American and white women participated in the civil rights movement, protesting racial discrimination. Women were also active in the student protests taking place on college campuses and in the antiwar movement that opposed United States involvement in the Vietnam War. Women involved in all these efforts, however, realized the men they worked with did not respect them or regard them as equals. The men took the leadership positions, while the women—instead of helping to make decisions—were expected to serve them. They were supposed to cook, clean, type, make coffee, and run the copy machines.

In 1964, Ruby Doris Smith-Robinson—a member of one of the leading civil rights groups, the Student Nonviolent Coordinating Committee (SNCC)—presented a paper called "The Position of Women in SNCC"

Below: Members of the National Organization for Women demonstrate in New York City. In 1967, the group adopted a "Bill of Rights for Women," which it planned to present to political candidates.

Above: Demonstrators against the Miss America Pageant on the boardwalk in Atlantic City. Women's rights campaigners felt that beauty pageants were degrading. They also criticized the message that little girls should want to grow up to be beauty queens rather than something more meaningful.

at a staff meeting. She stated that women were seen as second-class citizens in the fight to end segregation. SNCC's male leaders did not take her seriously. Women in other activist groups met with similar responses from male leaders when they demanded equality and respect. They realized that they would gain equality only when they organized on their own.

ACTIVIST GROUPS

Women began to form their own activist groups. The leading group was the National Organization for Women, set up in October 1966. The women (and some men) who founded NOW were frustrated by how slowly the United States government was acting against sex discrimination in employment. They doubted that government agencies were taking women's complaints seriously. They set up NOW to pursue the rights of women in the same way that the National Association for the Advancement of Colored People (NAACP) pursued rights for African Americans.

NOW took a mainstream approach, trusting that progress would be made in time through efforts to enforce existing laws or pass new

TURNING POINT

THE MISS AMERICA PROTEST

In 1968, the New York Radical Women staged a protest at the Miss America Pageant in Atlantic City, New Jersey. The protesters crowned a sheep as Miss America. They also tossed their bras, girdles, high heels, dishcloths, and other items into a "Freedom Trash Can." Although none of the women burned their bras, the event gave rise to the myth of feminist "bra burning." At the time, the Miss America Pageant was a major event, with millions of people watching the contest on television. As a result, the protest was widely reported in the media.

ones. More radical feminists, who were generally younger and tended to resist authority, did not want to rely on the government. They challenged institutions like the government, organized religion, universities, and the media, believing that they oppressed women. These feminists formed their own groups. The New York Radical Women and the Chicago Women's Liberation Group were both founded in 1967. (The Chicago group was the first to use the term "liberation" in connection with women's rights.) The Redstockings, who were mainly active in New York, followed two years later.

CONSCIOUSNESS RAISING

Women's liberation groups began to form throughout the United States. They held protest marches, staged demonstrations, and published newsletters. The members of the New York Radical Women began sharing their stories and personal experiences with one another in a process that came to be called "consciousness raising." The practice spread to many other women's groups. Consciousness raising played an important role in bringing women together as they realized that they had many common experiences.

THE PERSONAL IS POLITICAL

The phrase "the personal is political" became a rallying cry for the new feminists. It summarized the idea that many of the personal problems women experienced were not their fault but were the result of existing oppressive social and political systems. It also meant that what looked like personal problems were actually political issues, which could be solved if women became active and demanded solutions. For example, if a woman was worried on a personal level about finding someone to care for her children when she went to work, then the government could provide a solution by offering child care.

BREAKTHROUGH BIOGRAPHY

GLORIA STEINEM (1934–)

Gloria Steinem was born in Toledo, Ohio. After graduating from Smith College and studying abroad, she moved to New York in 1960 to become a writer. She also became active in the civil rights and antiwar movements. In 1969, Steinem attended a feminist "speakout" where women talked about their personal experiences with abortion, which was then illegal in the United States. Steinem had undergone an abortion years earlier, and she identified with the women. She quickly became active in the feminist movement and was soon its most visible voice and symbol. She played a leading role in numerous feminist groups and was one of the founders of *Ms.*, a magazine dedicated to women's issues. She continues to speak out and write on women's issues today.

Left: Gloria Steinem—shown at a demonstration against pornography—has long been one of the leading spokespeople for feminism.

Above: The cover of the preview issue of *Ms.* featured a woman with many arms holding an iron, frying pan, steering wheel, mirror, and other implements, to symbolize the numerous roles that housewives played.

TURNING POINT

MS. MAGAZINE APPEARS

Gloria Steinem and other feminists felt that women needed a national publication to provide information and bring women together. As a result, *Ms.* magazine was born. It first appeared as a special insert in *New York* magazine in December 1971. The first actual "preview" issue appeared in January 1972, and included articles with titles such as "Down with Sexist Upbringing," "Why Women Fear Success," and "How to Write Your Own Marriage Contract." Over succeeding years, *Ms.* published articles on a wide range of topics of interest to women.

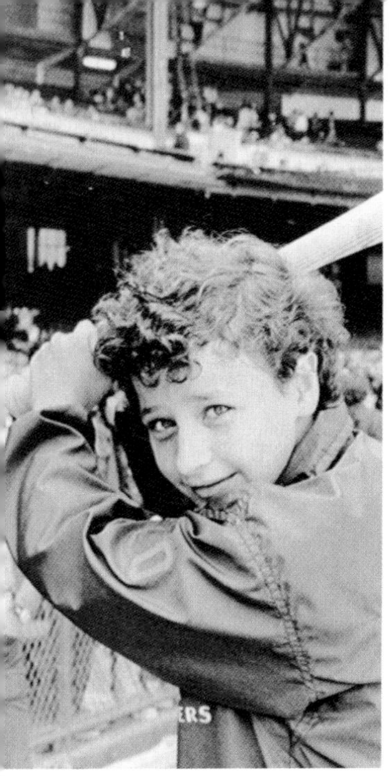

CHAPTER 3

DAILY LIFE

Aspects of daily life—including marriage and family, education, and sports—changed in many ways for women in the 1960s and 1970s. Traditional attitudes were challenged by various factors, including an increase in the divorce rate and a rise in the number of couples living together outside of marriage. Meanwhile, more women entered higher education and a greater number took part in competitive sports programs. A few women also achieved positions as religious leaders.

TURNING POINT

THE "NO-FAULT" DIVORCE LAW

In the early 1960s, most women assumed that marriage was for life. Divorce was frowned upon, and difficult to obtain. Almost every state required proof of bad behavior on the husband's part—such as cruelty or desertion—before granting a divorce. Then, in 1969, California passed a no-fault divorce law, which meant that a couple could divorce if the husband and wife were in agreement. Within five years, forty-four states had passed similar laws making it easier for couples to divorce. This led to a sharp increase in the number of divorces in the 1970s. In 1960, for example, there were 2.2 divorces for every 1,000 people. By 1980, the figure had risen to 5.2 per 1,000.

Above: Although new gadgets such as electric mixers reduced the time and effort required to do household chores, many women still felt trapped in their domestic role.

CHANGING ROLES

In the early 1960s, most households in the United States consisted of a man who went to work and a woman who stayed home and cared for the children. The majority of women were wives and mothers. They did not go to college or work at full-time careers. With the coming of the feminist movement, however, more women decided to attend college and enter the workforce. They also married at a later age and had fewer children.

Above: The makeup of the typical American family of the early 1960s—father, mother, and children—was increasingly challenged by changes in society.

Increasing numbers of families fell apart because of divorce. Marriage and the family were also changed by the rise of cohabitation, or people living together without getting married. In addition, more women chose to have children without getting married.

HOUSEWORK

Married women who went to work often discovered that they were still primarily responsible for doing the housework—buying groceries, cooking, washing dishes, cleaning, and doing laundry. The nature of housework had changed somewhat over the years, with the introduction of washing machines, clothes dryers, and dishwashers. There were also new convenience foods, so it took less time and effort to do household chores and prepare meals. If any married women hoped that their husbands would help out, they were disappointed. Men often claimed that they did not know how to cook or do laundry. After all, their mothers had done these chores, and their fathers had not helped out. Little by little, men began to take on some household chores, but the bulk of the housework was still done by women.

TURNING POINT

WOMEN ENTER THE SERVICE ACADEMIES

In 1976—as a result of a law passed by Congress the previous year—women for the first time entered the nation's military service academies, with more than three hundred enrolling at the U.S. Military, Naval, Air Force, and Coast Guard academies. The women who enlisted were not eligible for combat or for service on ships or aircraft engaged in combat missions, even though they received training for such roles. Nevertheless, the women proved themselves capable of meeting the rigorous standards and tough training of the military.

SINGLE-SEX SCHOOLS GO COED

Some of the most prestigious colleges in the United States were founded as male-only institutions. Many feminists argued that women should be able to attend these schools, and in 1969, Yale—one of the elite colleges—began admitting women undergraduates. In the next few years, other men's schools, such as Princeton and Brown, did the same. There were also excellent all-female colleges; one group was known as the Seven Sisters. In 1969, one of the Seven Sisters—Vassar—began admitting men. Another of the Seven Sisters, Radcliffe, reached an agreement with Harvard in 1977 that led them to merge several years later. Some feminists maintained that women got a better education in all-female schools, which provided them with a more supportive learning environment.

HIGHER EDUCATION

An increasing number of women pursued higher education, so that by 1978, for the first time, more women than men enrolled in college. However, female students soon discovered that their classes were taught from a male perspective, which did not include the views or roles of women. They began to demand classes with a female emphasis. In 1970, San Diego State University in California offered the first official women's studies program. By 1973, there were seventy-eight such programs, and by 1977 there were 276. In addition, many colleges that did not have full programs offered separate courses in women's studies.

Women also began to gain more professional degrees. In 1970, for example, women received only 8.4 percent of medical degrees, but by 1980 the figure had risen to 23.4 percent. Dental degrees earned by women jumped from 0.9 percent in 1970 to 13.3 percent in 1980. Law degrees rose from 5.4 percent in 1970 to 30.2 percent in 1980.

Inequalities remained, however: women made up a minority of professors at colleges and universities, and they tended to be

Below: Some married women decided to return to school. These not altogether convincing photographs show a female student in Massachusetts, who brought her baby to college when she could not find a sitter.

Left: Yale University students gather at a political protest in May 1970. Women had been admitted to Yale—once an all-male institution—the year before.

employed at lower levels than men—instructors, for example, rather than full professors. Women also earned less than men and had a harder time getting promoted.

SCHOOL SPORTS

Women had long been discouraged from participating in rigorous sports. In 1961, nine states even prohibited interscholastic sports for girls. Very few girls participated in high-school sports, and there were practically no college scholarships for female athletes. This situation changed with the passage of Title IX of the Education Amendments of 1972. Title IX prohibited sex discrimination in educational institutions that received federal funds. Its most significant effect was that high

NO MORE EXCUSES

"These are the bodies Yale is exploiting. We have come here today to make clear how unprotected we are. . . . On a day like today the rain freezes on our skin. Then we sit on a bus for half an hour as the ice melts into our sweats. . . . No effective action has been taken and no matter what we hear, it doesn't make these bodies warmer, or dryer or less prone to sickness. We can't accept any excuses, nor can we trust to normal channels of complaint, since the need for lockers for the women's crew [rowing team] has existed since last spring. . . . We are not just healthy young things in blue and white uniforms who perform feats of strength for Yale in the nice spring weather; we are not just statistics on your win column. We're human and being treated as less than such."

A statement read by the captain of the Yale University women's rowing team during a 1976 protest. Despite Title IX, the women did not have showers or locker rooms.

WOMEN OF COURAGE AND CONVICTION

KATHRINE SWITZER (1947–)

Kathrine Switzer began running when she was twelve years old. She trained with the men's track team at Syracuse University since there was no women's team. She decided to enter the Boston Marathon—one of the most famous long-distance races in the world. Women were not allowed to enter, since they were believed to be too weak to run 26.2 miles (42.2 kilometers). But in 1966 a woman named Roberta Gibb had hidden in the bushes near the starting line and slipped into the pack. In 1967, Switzer officially entered the race as "K. Switzer," wearing a sweatsuit with a hood to cover her face. When a race official realized she was a woman, he tried to stop her, but Switzer's boyfriend blocked him, and she finished the race. Women were finally allowed to run officially in Boston in 1972, and Switzer finished third among them. She also won the New York Marathon in 1974.

Above: A race official (in street clothes) tries to stop Kathrine Switzer (wearing #261) from running in the 1967 Boston Marathon. A male runner blocked him, and Switzer was able to complete the race.

schools and colleges were required to give women's sports programs the same funding as men's programs.

Title IX immediately increased female participation in sports programs. In 1997, the U.S. Department of Education issued a report called "Title IX: 25 Years of Progress." It showed that in 1971 only about 300,000 high-school girls, representing 7.5 percent of students, were involved in school sports programs. By 1996 that number had risen to 2.4 million, or 39 percent of students. In 1972, women made up only 15 percent of college athletes, whereas in 1995 they represented 37 percent.

Left: Despite rules that only boys could play Little League ball, Maria Pepe pitched in three games for a New Jersey team in 1972. Eventually, after a successful lawsuit filed by NOW, girls were allowed to take part in Little League.

LITTLE LEAGUE

In 1950, young Kathryn Johnston disguised herself as a boy and made the Little League team in Corning, New York, becoming the first girl to play Little League ball. The next year, however, the Little League Baseball organization officially ruled that only boys could play. Despite this, in 1972, twelve-year-old Maria Pepe made the team in Hoboken, New Jersey, and pitched in three games. The Little League organization threatened to revoke (take back) the team's charter unless she left the team. NOW brought a discrimination lawsuit against Little League on behalf of Pepe and other New Jersey girls. Sylvia Pressler, a judge for the state Division of Civil Rights, ruled in favor of the girls. Her decision was then upheld by a higher court, and in 1974, Little League agreed to let girls play. Within days, eleven-year-old Bunny Taylor of Clay, West Virginia, had pitched a no-hitter for her Little League team. Little League also set up a separate softball program for girls.

WORKING FOR EQUALITY IN RELIGION

Women were limited in the roles they could play in the major religions in the United States. They could not, for example, become priests in

TURNING POINT

THE "BATTLE OF THE SEXES"

Bobby Riggs, a fifty-five-year-old tennis player, said that since men were physically and mentally stronger than women he could beat even the world's best female player. Professional player Billie Jean King, who was twenty-nine and at the top of her game, took up his challenge. On September 20, 1973, the two met at the Houston Astrodome in what became known as the Battle of the Sexes. In front of a huge television audience, King beat Riggs easily in three straight sets. Her victory is regarded as one of the most important moments in women's sports. King—a passionate, aggressive player—had long fought for equality and respect for women athletes. She succeeded in getting tournaments to award equal prize money to women and cofounded the Women's Sports Foundation in 1974.

BREAKTHROUGH BIOGRAPHY

MARY DALY (1928–2010)
Mary Daly was born in Schenectady, New York. She earned three doctoral degrees in theology (religion) and philosophy. Daly began teaching at Boston College, a Catholic institution, in 1966. Two years later, she published *The Church and the Second Sex*, in which she stated that the Catholic Church had oppressed women for hundreds of years. In what was widely seen as a response to the book, Daly was denied tenure by the college in 1969, but was reinstated after more than 1,500 students signed a petition supporting her. Daly—who described herself as a "radical lesbian feminist"—wrote many other books, including *Beyond God the Father: Toward a Philosophy of Women's Liberation* (1973). She eventually decided that organized religion would never stop being male-dominated.

the Roman Catholic Church or rabbis in the Jewish faith. Only certain Protestant denominations ordained women as church leaders. Feminists sought a more equal role in both leadership and worship activities.

PROTESTANTISM

An increasing number of Protestant groups began ordaining women in the 1970s—but sometimes not until after a struggle. In 1970 and 1973, the General Convention of the Episcopal Church voted against ordaining women. In 1974, eleven women were unofficially ordained—a development the Church declared invalid. Two years later, however, the General Convention passed a resolution declaring that "no one shall be denied access" to ordination on the basis of sex. By the end of 1977, one hundred women had been ordained in the Episcopal Church. Meanwhile, in the Lutheran Church in the United States, rules were changed in 1970 to allow the ordination of women. On November

Right: The Lutheran Church allowed the ordination of women in 1970. Here, in 1977, Janith Otte-Murphy becomes one of the first women to be ordained.

22, 1970, Elizabeth Alvina Platz made headlines as the first woman to be ordained into the Lutheran ministry in North America.

JUDAISM

Sally Jean Priesand was ordained as the first woman rabbi in the United States on June 3, 1972. Priesand was a Reform Jew—the most liberal of the different movements that make up Judaism. Sandy Eisenberg Sasso was ordained in the modern Reconstructionist movement in 1974. Jewish women also wanted to be counted in a "minyan"—the minimum number of ten adult Jews required for a religious ceremony. Reform and Reconstructionist Jews had included women as part of a minyan for years; conservative Jews began counting them in 1973.

CATHOLICISM

The Roman Catholic Church was more resistant to change. The National Coalition of American Nuns was founded in 1969 to work for female equality, but the Pope was reluctant to grant them a formal role in the ministry. In 1976, the Catholic Church issued a declaration stating that women could not become priests. When Pope John Paul II visited the United States in 1979, Sister Mary Theresa Kane appealed to him before a large crowd in Washington, D.C. She asked him to consider the ordination of "half of humankind." The Catholic Church has still not changed its official stand on the issue.

TURNING POINT

THE WOMEN STRIKE FOR PEACE

Some women in the early 1960s looked beyond their traditional roles and took a stand on world developments. On November 1, 1961, an organization called the Women Strike for Peace staged a walkout by 50,000 women, most of them young, white, middle-class housewives. They were upset about tensions between the United States and the Soviet Union and at both countries' development of dangerous nuclear weapons. The women called for a ban on the development and testing of such weapons. Their motto was "End the arms race—not the human race."

Right: The campaign for women's rights had a long history of collaboration with the anti-war movement. In the 1960s, American singer and social activist Joan Baez was outspoken in her opposition to the Vietnam War. She is pictured here (at left) with her sister Mimi Fariña, also a peace activist, performing at the Newport Folk Festival in 1967.

CHAPTER 4

Politics and the Law

FEMINISTS REALIZED THAT IF THEY WANTED CHANGE, they needed to become more involved in the political process. In the 1960s and 1970s many women got involved, and an increasing number were elected to public office. Their efforts failed, however, to get an important piece of legislation passed—the Equal Rights Amendment.

WOMEN OF COURAGE AND CONVICTION

SHIRLEY CHISHOLM (1924–2005)

Shirley Chisholm was born in Brooklyn, New York. After earning an MA from Columbia University, she became a teacher and directed a child-care center, then served in the New York State Assembly from 1964 to 1968. While there, she was known for her interest in education and the problems of domestic workers. In 1968, she became the first African-American woman elected to Congress. Chisholm was reelected to the House five times. In Congress, she was a fervent supporter of poor, minority, and female Americans. In 1972, she became the first woman and the first African-American woman to run for president in the Democratic primaries.

WOMEN IN PUBLIC OFFICE

The National Women's Political Caucus (NWPC) was formed in 1971. Its purpose was to get more women involved in public life—not only as officeholders but also as committee members, judges, and delegates to the national conventions at which presidential candidates were nominated. NWPC set out to identify, recruit, and train women

Right: One of the leading feminists in Congress, Bella Abzug—shown wearing one of her trademark hats—served three terms, beginning in 1971.

for these roles and to help raise money for them. Gloria Steinem, Betty Friedan, and Fannie Lou Hamer were among the founders of the group, which included women from both major political parties.

A number of women served in Congress during these years, many of them blazing new trails as "firsts." In 1964, Patsy Takemoto Mink was the first Asian-American woman and the first woman of color elected to Congress. In 1968, Shirley Chisholm was the first African-American woman, and in 1970, Bella Abzug was the first Jewish woman elected to Congress. These women were strong supporters of women's rights during their many years in Washington, D.C.

FEMALE SENATORS

In 1971, when NWPC was formed, there were few women in government at the national, state, and local levels. Between 1971 and 1973, out of a total of one hundred, only two women were in the U.S. Senate—Margaret Chase Smith and Elaine Edwards. Edwards had not even been elected. Her husband, the governor of Louisiana, had appointed her to fill the seat temporarily when the existing senator had died suddenly. Meanwhile, there were thirteen women in the House of Representatives out of a total of 435 members. The numbers had changed little by 1981, when one woman—Nancy Landon Kassebaum—was in the Senate and sixteen were in the House. Kassebaum was the first woman elected to the Senate who was not the widow of a congressman.

GOVERNORS AND LEGISLATORS

There were no women governors in 1971. In 1974, the Democrat Ella Grasso was elected governor of Connecticut. She was the first woman to be elected governor on her own, without having succeeded her husband. Dixy Lee Ray, a marine biologist and former

TURNING POINT

A WOMAN IS NOMINATED FOR PRESIDENT

Senator Margaret Chase Smith became the first woman nominated for president by a major political party at the 1964 Republican convention. Smith had entered the House of Representatives in 1940 to complete the term of her husband, who had died. She then ran for the seat herself and served in the House for eight years, until she was elected to the Senate in 1948. In January 1964, Smith announced her candidacy for president, becoming the first woman ever to seek the presidential nomination of a major party. At the Republican convention in July, she received the votes of twenty-seven delegates but lost the nomination to Senator Barry Goldwater.

Below: Senator Margaret Chase Smith of Maine, shown at the 1964 Republican national convention.

TURNING POINT

THE WOMEN'S STRIKE FOR EQUALITY

More than 100,000 women across the United States held rallies during the Women's Strike for Equality, which was organized by NOW on August 26, 1970. The date marked the fiftieth anniversary of women's suffrage. Betty Friedan had called for such a demonstration to prove that women widely supported feminist efforts. She led a march of 50,000 people in New York City. At a huge rally, Gloria Steinem announced the march's goals: improved child care, reproductive rights, and equality in jobs and education. Feminists also hung a 40-foot (12-meter) sign on the Statue of Liberty reading "Women of the World Unite!"

Right: The Statue of Liberty was decorated by feminists with a banner supporting women's rights in August 1970.

head of the Atomic Energy Commission, was elected governor of Washington in 1976.

Women had more success being elected to state legislatures. In 1971, there were 344 women legislators, representing 4.5 percent of the total. In 1979, the number rose to 770 women, or 10.3 percent. In other statewide positions—such as lieutenant governor, attorney general, and secretary of state—representation by women increased from twenty-four in 1971 (7.0 percent) to thirty-five in 1979 (10.7 percent).

A PRESENCE AT THE CONVENTIONS

Every four years, the Democratic and Republican parties hold national conventions where they nominate their presidential candidates and outline their principles and goals. Conventions, which are shown on television, are also important for symbolic reasons. They give each party the opportunity to show the public what they think is important—for

Above: Activist Angela Davis (center, seated) at a press conference in 1972, after her release on bail. Davis, accused of supplying a weapon used in a shootout, had been held in jail for more than a year. She was eventually found not guilty.

example, by the type of people who attend the conventions as delegates and by the individuals who are asked to make speeches.

Women began to play an increasing role at the conventions. At the 1968 Democratic convention, women made up only 13 percent of the delegates. By 1972—as a result of guidelines written to ensure that there was better representation of women, minorities, and young people—women made up 40 percent of delegates. The proportion of women at the 1976 Democratic convention dropped to 33 percent, but in 1978, the Democrats passed standards requiring that as of the 1980 convention, half the delegates would have to be women.

Women also became more involved in the Republican conventions. While only 16 percent of delegates at the 1968 convention were

BREAKTHROUGH BIOGRAPHY

ANGELA DAVIS (1944–)

Angela Davis has been a college professor, a member of the Communist Party, an African-American rights activist, and has belonged to the radical group the Black Panthers. In 1970 she was accused of supplying a gun used in a courtroom shootout in which four people were killed and two African-American prisoners tried to escape. Davis went on the run and was placed on the FBI's most wanted list. After she was caught, she was charged with conspiracy, murder, and kidnapping and held in jail for more than a year before finally being put on trial. Meanwhile, a "Free Angela" campaign was organized by people who were angry at her treatment. She was found not guilty in 1972. Davis became a university professor in California, wrote numerous books, and is still active in women's and minority issues.

TURNING POINT

THE NATIONAL WOMEN'S CONFERENCE

The National Women's Conference was held in Houston, Texas, on November 18–21, 1977 to celebrate women, evaluate their status, and decide on future goals. It involved 2,000 delegates (most elected at fifty-six state and territorial meetings) of remarkable diversity: 35 percent were nonwhite, for example, and 20 percent were low income. Bella Abzug presided over the conference, which was also attended by Betty Friedan, Gloria Steinem, first lady Rosalyn Carter, and former first ladies Lady Bird Johnson and Betty Ford. The delegates agreed on a "National Plan of Action," including passage of the ERA, the right to abortion, and a national health plan with specific provisions for women. Some of these provisions were controversial. A significant number of delegates, for example, were opposed to the ERA and abortion.

women, the figure rose to 29 percent in 1972 and 31 percent in 1976. The party subsequently ruled that at least one-third of all delegates would be women. Individual women also became more prominent. In 1972, Anne Armstrong, who was active in Texas politics, became the first woman ever to deliver the keynote address (one of the most important speeches) at a national presidential convention. She also became the first woman to co-chair the Republican convention.

THE EQUAL RIGHTS AMENDMENT

If women had success in some areas, they failed in their attempt to pass the Equal Rights Amendment (ERA), a proposed addition to the U.S. Constitution. The text of the amendment—designed to make the equality of men and women part of the Constitution—read "Equality under the law shall not be denied or abridged by the United States or by any State on account of sex." The amendment was first proposed in 1923 and was regularly reintroduced in Congress over the years. It was finally passed by Congress in March 1972. Before it could become part of the Constitution, though, it needed

Below: Feminists march in New York City on August 26, 1970, during the Women's Strike for Equality. The date was the fiftieth anniversary of the passage of the 19th Amendment, giving women the right to vote.

Left: Thousands rallied in Springfield, Illinois, in May 1976 in support of the Equal Rights Amendment. Despite such efforts, the ERA was not ratified (agreed) by the required number of states.

to be sent to the state legislatures for ratification (formal approval). Thirty-eight states needed to approve the amendment within seven years. Hawaii's state legislature ratified the ERA within thirty minutes of its passage by Congress. By 1977, thiry-five states had ratified it.

However, soon after the ERA was passed by Congress, efforts began to stop it at the state level. Phyllis Schlafly, a conservative activist, organized the most effective group, called STOP ERA. She and other ERA opponents said that the amendment was unfair to women. They warned that if the amendment was ratified it would mean that women would be drafted and sent into combat, forced to work even if they did not want to, denied alimony (financial support) in the event of divorce, and required to share public restrooms with men. Another factor working against the ERA's passage was the fact that

WOMEN OF COURAGE AND CONVICTION

MAGGIE KUHN (1905–95)

Margaret Kuhn was born in Buffalo, New York. She was a lifelong activist, involved in civil rights, labor union efforts, and women's rights. In 1970 she became involved in another movement—for the rights of older people. That year, when she turned sixty-five, Kuhn was forced to leave her job with the United Presbyterian Church in New York because she had reached the set retirement age. Then, with five other women who had also been forced to retire, she started the Gray Panthers, an advocacy group to protest ageism (prejudice based on age) and ensure the rights of older people. The Gray Panthers succeeded in raising the retirement age to seventy. They also looked at conditions in nursing homes, patients' rights, and health care and sought better portrayals of older people in the media.

men made up the vast majority of state legislators, who cast the votes on the amendment.

As the 1979 deadline for ratification came near, Congress in 1978 voted to extend the date. When the new deadline arrived on June 30, 1982, however, three states still needed to ratify the ERA.

WOMEN TAKE THEIR PLACE ON JURIES

Juries are an important part of the U.S. judicial system. They decide the outcome of trials and see that justice is done. Until the 1970s, however, women often did not serve on juries because they were discouraged or prevented from doing so. As the vast majority of jurors was male, it meant that women's views were not considered and that women were not participating in an important part of the judicial system. Three

BREAKTHROUGH BIOGRAPHY

PHYLLIS SCHLAFLY (1924–)

Phyllis Schlafly was born in St. Louis, Missouri. She graduated from Washington University in 1944, received a master's degree in government in 1945, and eventually earned a law degree in 1978. She got married in 1949 and had six children. Schlafly said a woman's most important career was to be a housewife and mother, but she never limited herself to such roles. She became active in Republican politics and ran unsuccessfully for Congress. In 1967, she founded the conservative newsletter the *Phyllis Schlafly Report*. Her main focus at the time was national defense and military issues. She later founded STOP ERA and the Eagle Forum and became the major opponent of the ERA and leader of the antifeminist movement. Schlafly continues to speak out for traditional family roles and values and against such issues as abortion and gay rights.

Right: Phyllis Schlafly holding a "STOP ERA" cushion. Schlafly described herself as a "housewife" and called her political career as arch-opponent to the Equal Rights Amendment a "hobby."

states (Alabama, Mississippi, and South Carolina) prohibited women from serving, and other states made it very difficult for them. Some states made it very easy for women not to serve.

In 1961, the Supreme Court (in the case of *Hoyt v. Florida*) ruled in favor of a Florida law requiring women to register in order to serve on juries. Few women registered and asked to serve. Meanwhile, men were automatically registered for jury duty, so all-male juries were usual in Florida. It was not until 1975 that the Court (in the case of *Taylor v. Louisiana*) ruled that it was unconstitutional to make women register for jury service. Justice Byron White wrote that juries must be selected even-handedly from a representative cross-section of the community—in other words, women as well as men.

THE GOVERNMENT RECOGNIZES "MS."

The Government Printing Office officially authorized the use of the term "Ms." in federal publications in 1972. For most of the 20th century, women were referred to as "Miss" or "Mrs."—terms that clearly indicated their marital status. Meanwhile, "Mr." did not indicate anything about a man's marital status. Over the years, various people had suggested Ms. as a suitable title for women. In 1961, a New Yorker named Sheila Michaels began to publicize the use of Ms., which became popular with feminists.

Below: Thousands of women—and some men as well—took part in the National Women's Conference in November 1977, including leading feminists, the current first lady, and two former first ladies.

CHAPTER 5

The World of Work

By 1960, one-third of American women were in the workforce. They were used to earning much less than men; after all, most people believed that men were the family breadwinners. Employers often assumed that their female employees were either single and living with their parents, or married and working only to earn "pin money"—not to support their families. Many women, however, were working because they needed to. In addition, women had fewer opportunities than men, since they were either discouraged or prevented from doing many jobs.

Right: Feminists wore buttons such as these to demand the same pay as men for doing the same work. In 1963, women earned only 59¢ for every dollar earned by men.

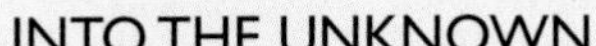

INTO THE UNKNOWN

"The entering class [at law school] was 20 percent women—a previously unheard of proportion. . . . In making the decision to apply to law school, we were stepping out of our comfort zones. Ours was a generation groomed to be housewives, teachers, secretaries, or nurses. Not one of us women arrived at law school . . . with a lifelong ambition of becoming an attorney; this was not an avenue normally presented to women of our generation."

Retired attorney Elizabeth Langer, on her entry to Rutgers Law School in 1970

MARRIED WOMEN

Whether they worked or not, women had only limited independence in financial matters. In many states, married women were restricted in their ability to sign contracts, sell property, engage in business, make wills, or control their own earnings. Their husbands made the decisions and signed all the papers.

Among the leading demands of the second wave of feminists were equal pay, equal work opportunities, and financial independence. New laws and legal decisions made during the 1960s and 1970s meant that many of these demands were met. In 1975, *Time* magazine was celebrating the successes of the feminist movement. Women had come to see that there were many jobs they could have, and ambitions they could realize.

TURNING POINT

OFFICE WORKERS' REVOLT

Iris Rivera, a legal secretary in Chicago, Illinois, was fired in 1977 after refusing to make coffee every morning for her boss. Rivera said she didn't drink coffee herself, that making coffee was not part of her job description, and that "ordering the secretaries to fix the coffee is taking the role of homemaker too far." The next day, during their lunch hour, fifty other secretaries protested in downtown Chicago, and newspapers and radio stations turned out to cover the event. Rivera—a widow and the mother of three sons—got her job back, but clerical workers staged other demonstrations. Groups such as Women Employed, 9 to 5, and Working Women: The National Association for Office Workers protested the ways in which male employers were disrespectful to female workers and how such behavior made them feel inferior.

Left: Secretary Iris Rivera with a copy of the notice firing her in 1977. Rivera had refused to make coffee for her boss.

LEGISLATION AND LAWS

The Equal Pay Act of 1963 was one of the most important laws passed in the 1960s. Signed into legislation by President Kennedy, it was the first federal law to prohibit discrimination based on sex. The Equal Pay Act said that private employers had to give men and women equal pay for doing the same jobs under the same conditions. The act was not perfect however: it did not, for instance, cover domestic workers or women in executive, professional, or administrative positions. Parts of the law were also open to different interpretations.

CIVIL RIGHTS AND EQUAL OPPORTUNITIES

The Civil Rights Act of 1964 was another important piece of legislation. It included a part called Title VII, which prohibited

Above: President Lyndon Johnson (front) signs the Civil Rights Act of 1964 into law.

TURNING POINT

THE CIVIL RIGHTS ACT INCLUDES WOMEN

It was never intended that sex discrimination should be covered by the Civil Rights Act of 1964. Many legislators opposed the passage of such sweeping civil rights legislation, including Democratic Representative Howard W. Smith, a conservative opponent of civil rights. In an effort to try to defeat the entire bill, Smith suggested adding discrimination based on sex to Title VII. He assumed his colleagues would not think sex discrimination was a serious issue, so they would vote against the bill. Smith was wrong. When the measure passed the House, a woman sitting in the gallery shouted, "We made it! God bless America!" Guards then escorted her outside.

employment discrimination—including hiring and promotion—on the basis of race, color, religion, sex, or national origin. The Equal Employment Opportunity Commission (EEOC) was set up to enforce the law. The EEOC had no actual power, though, and the law did not cover government employees, teachers, and women in the military. Moreover, the EEOC saw its main role as preventing discrimination based on race—not sex. Despite this, one-third of the complaints filed with the EEOC in its first year involved sex discrimination.

Feminists criticized the EEOC for working too slowly. (Frustration with the EEOC was one of the major reasons for the founding of NOW.) Also, the EEOC's guidelines said that employers could discriminate against women if gender was shown to be a "bona fide occupational qualification," or BFOQ. For example, it would be necessary to hire a man as opposed to a woman as an attendant in a men's restroom. However, this meant that employers could use the BFOQ standard legally to discriminate against women.

SLOW PROGRESS

Slowly but surely, progress was made in expanding women's rights in employment and other financial matters. As a result of pressure from

NOW, President Lyndon Johnson issued two Executive Orders, in 1965 and 1967, to ban sex discrimination in employment by the federal government and by employers holding contracts from the federal government. Both the federal government and its contractors were told to take affirmative action to overcome discrimination based on sex, race, color, religion, or national origin.

In 1972, Congress passed the Equal Employment Opportunity Act, which enabled the EEOC to sue in federal courts when it uncovered employment discrimination. The law extended to educational institutions, small businesses, and federal and state employees. In 1974, the Equal Credit Opportunity Act was passed. Businesses—including banks, credit-card

TURNING POINT

THE IMAGE OF FLIGHT ATTENDANTS CHANGES

In the early 1960s, flight attendants were all young, single, attractive women who were referred to as stewardesses. They could be fired if they turned thirty-two or thirty-five (depending on the airline) or if they got married. They were frequently weighed to make sure they maintained their slim figures. Title VII of the Civil Rights Act gave stewardesses the opportunity to challenge such policies, and they were among the first to file complaints with the EEOC. The women also resented the way airlines portrayed them as sexual objects for male passengers, with such advertising slogans as "I'm Cheryl. Fly me." In 1968, the EEOC prohibited airlines from discriminating against older and/or married women. The EEOC also ruled that being female was not a job requirement, so men could be hired as flight attendants, too.

Below: An airline flight attendant chats with a passenger in 1968. Flight attendants—who were all women at the time—often resented the way they were treated by their employers.

Above: Pilot Jerrie Cobb, shown in 1960, undergoing a stress resistance test. She took many tests to become an astronaut and passed them all, but the National Aeronautics and Space Administration canceled its women's program in 1963. The United States did not send a woman into space until 1982.

WOMEN OF COURAGE AND CONVICTION

JERRIE COBB (1931–)

Geraldyn Cobb was born in Norman, Oklahoma. Fascinated with flight, she got her pilot's license on her seventeenth birthday. While working as a commercial pilot in 1959, she met Dr. W. Randolph Lovelace, who was advising the newly formed National Aeronautics and Space Administration (NASA). Lovelace asked Cobb if she could be his first test subject for research on the effects of space flight on women, to see if women were physically and mentally capable of becoming astronauts. In 1960 and 1961, Cobb and a number of other women were tested. Thirteen women, including Cobb, passed, but then NASA stopped the tests. In June 1963, the Soviet Union sent a woman, Valentina Tereshkova, into space. The next month, Cobb went before a Congressional committee to argue that the United States should also have women astronauts. Despite this, NASA canceled its women's program. Cobb then turned her attention to piloting missionary flights to South America. It was not until 1978 that NASA named its first six women astronauts and not until 1982 that an American woman—Sally Ride—went into space.

companies, and mortgage lenders—could no longer discriminate against women because of their sex or marital status.

LABOR LAWS

The courts also played a part in expanding women's rights in employment and financial matters. In 1968, a federal district court ruled against so-called protective labor laws (instituted to "protect" women from things that were considered unsuitable or unsafe) in California. These laws prevented women from working overtime or lifting heavy objects. In 1969, two other important decisions struck down similar laws excluding women from jobs that involved lifting weights of more than 30 pounds (13.6 kilograms). In 1971, the Supreme Court overturned an Idaho law that gave a man preference to act as the executor (administrator) of the estate of an individual who

Left: Labor activist Mary Moultrie (left) stands alongside Reverend Ralph Abernathy during a 1969 hospital workers' strike in Charleston, South Carolina. The strikers demanded higher pay for low-income workers.

had died. The same year, the Court ruled that a company could not refuse to hire the mothers of young children unless it refused to hire the fathers, too.

PREGNANT WORKERS

Pregnancy was often seen as a condition that made it impossible for women to work, rather than a time when women could continue their usual activities. In 1972, the EEOC released guidelines stating that employers could not fire workers when they became pregnant or force pregnant workers to take leaves of absence. Two years later, in the case of *Cleveland Board of Education v. LaFleur*, the Supreme Court ruled that it was illegal to force pregnant women to take maternity leave. The case involved the school board of Cleveland, Ohio, which required pregnant teachers to take five months of unpaid maternity leave before their babies were due.

"HELP WANTED" ADS NO LONGER DIVIDED BY SEX

It had long been common practice for "help wanted" ads in newspapers to be divided into "male" and "female" categories. In 1968—after two years of pressure from NOW—the EEOC ruled that the practice was illegal because it violated the Civil Rights Act of 1964. (If gender was regarded as a BFOQ, ads could specify male or female.) Specific newspapers did not always follow the guidelines, though, and the American Newspaper Publishers Association filed a lawsuit against the EEOC and its ruling. In 1973, the Supreme Court upheld the ruling, opening the way for women to apply for jobs that had previously been advertised only to men.

WOMEN OF COURAGE AND CONVICTION

DOLORES HUERTA (1930–)

Dolores Huerta was born in Dawson, New Mexico, and grew up in Stockton, California. Huerta entered community service, dedicated to improving the conditions of migrant farm workers and helping them gain economic, political, and social rights. In 1962, she helped found the United Farm Workers with César Chávez. To help the farm workers negotiate for better conditions, she played a major role in mounting national boycotts of California grape and lettuce growers. Meanwhile, she raised eleven children (whom she often brought with her to the picket lines), was beaten by union busters, and was arrested some twenty times.

Below: Dolores Huerta continues to work today to help the working poor, women, and children.

In 1978, Congress passed the Pregnancy Discrimination Act, which made pregnant women eligible to receive the same type of disability pay or leave time given to workers with other types of temporary conditions. The law also meant that employers could not question women who were applying for jobs about their plans to have children.

ORGANIZING AND UNIONIZING

Efforts were made to organize women workers in a number of fields to help them fight for better conditions and pay. As more women entered the workforce, more of them joined labor unions. In 1974, women from fifty-eight different unions formed the Coalition of Labor Union Women. The coalition aimed to get more women into unions and strengthen their role there, in addition to promoting affirmative action in the workplace.

Efforts were mounted in specific cases to improve the conditions for working women. In 1969, for example, 400 hospital workers in Charleston, South Carolina—almost all of them women, and all African American—went on strike for 113 days to gain recognition (official approval) for their union. The workers were led by Mary Ann Moultrie, a twenty-four-year-old African-American nursing assistant, who said they went on strike: "so that we could win the right to be treated as human beings." In 1974, Crystal Lee Jordan—a thirty-three-year-old mother of three who was earning only $2.65 per hour—attempted to organize thousands of textile workers at a J.P. Stevens plant in Roanoke Rapids, North Carolina. The company fired her. However, a year later the workers succeeded in unionizing. Jordan's story became the basis of the 1979 movie *Norma Rae*.

Above: As a result of gains made during the 1960s and 1970s, women could join the military and have nontraditional careers.

By the 1970s, new careers were open for women. They could become jet pilots, FBI agents, engineers, and steelworkers. Many remained in traditionally "female" occupations, however, and there were still relatively few women in top executive positions.

WOMEN OF COURAGE AND CONVICTION

BRENDA BERKMAN
(1951–)

Brenda Berkman graduated from St. Olaf College in Minnesota in 1973. She had always wanted to be a firefighter. When she was in law school at New York University in 1977, the New York City fire department began taking applications from women, and she applied. However, none of the women who applied passed the physical strength test, because it had been designed for men. Berkman filed a lawsuit against the city of New York, charging that the test was biased against women and did not fairly evaluate their potential firefighting skills. In 1982, a judge ruled that the test had discriminated against women. That year, Berkman passed the revised test and became one of the first female firefighters. She retired in 2006 and became an artist.

CHAPTER 6

Health and Sexuality

The 1960s marked the dawning of the sexual revolution, a development that some people considered shocking but others found liberating and exciting. Birth control, abortion and gay rights became important issues, as did the recognition that women needed protecting from violence.

TURNING POINT

ACCESS TO CONTRACEPTIVES

In the 1960s, many states had laws limiting the advertising or sale of contraceptives. However, with the advent of the Pill, the decade witnessed a great deal of social change involving birth control. In 1965, the Supreme Court issued a ruling in the case of *Griswold v. Connecticut*, overturning a state law against providing contraceptives to married people. Seven years later, in the case of *Eisenstadt v. Baird,* the Court said that single people also had the same right to birth control.

THE PILL

The oral contraceptive—which came to be known simply as the Pill—was approved for use in the United States in 1960. Within a few years, millions of women were using it to prevent pregnancy. There were other methods of contraception, but none was as convenient or reliable as the Pill. It was simple to use, could be taken privately, and was completely under a woman's control. At a time when many young people were rebelling against the customs and practices of their elders, women

Right: Hippies dancing at a festival in New Orleans, Louisiana. A new age dawned during the late 1960s when a counterculture of music, clothing, and attitudes was born.

could now engage in sexual activity without the fear of becoming pregnant. All this helped lead to the sexual revolution of the late 1960s.

ATTITUDES TOWARD SEX

One idea behind the sexual revolution was that women, like men, had sexual needs—an extreme view at the time. People began to talk openly about sex and engage in sexual activity at a younger age, sometimes before marriage. Conservatives feared that the American family was being threatened, and many people were disturbed because the new attitudes challenged the "double standard" that held it was acceptable for single men to have sex but not single women. Women now wanted this sexual freedom as well.

Helen Gurley Brown did much to promote such freedom. In 1962, she published *Sex and the Single Girl*—a scandalous bestseller about young, single, sexually active working women. Three years later, Brown became the editor of *Cosmopolitan* magazine, which published articles on fashion, sex, and the workplace. Its many independent, ambitious readers may not have been feminists in the strict sense, but they certainly were not willing to settle for traditional roles. "*Cosmo* is feminist in that we believe women are just as smart and capable as men are and can achieve anything men can," Brown said. "But it also acknowledges that while work is important, men are, too."

THE BATTLE OVER ABORTION

Abortion (the termination of pregnancy) was one of the most heated issues of the 1960s and 1970s. In most of the United

TURNING POINT

NEW VIEWS OF MENOPAUSE

All in the Family was a popular television show in the 1970s. In one 1972 episode, the character Edith Bunker began having wild mood swings as she went through menopause, which was referred to as "change of life." Edith's doctor gave her some pills to take. They were probably hormones, which were widely prescribed for women going through menopause. Views of menopause were shaped by practitioners such as Dr. Robert A. Wilson, who wrote the book *Feminine Forever* (1966). Wilson did not see menopause as a normal stage of a woman's life but as a disease that could be cured with hormones. He called aging women "flabby," "shrunken," and "dull-minded." Many middle-aged and older women took hormones, even after studies in the mid-1970s noted their connection to certain kinds of cancer.

Right: *Cosmopolitan* magazine, edited by Helen Gurley Brown (shown here in 1966), appealed to independent, ambitious women who were frank about liking men.

States, abortion was a crime, so women who wished to end a pregnancy had few choices. They were either forced to seek out illegal and often dangerous procedures or travel outside the United States to where abortions were more readily available—and the latter was an option only for women who could afford it. Thousands of women died each year as a result of illegal abortions. Many women began to call for changes in the laws to make abortion legal, on the grounds that women had the right to control their own bodies and decide whether and when to have children.

LIBERALIZATION, OR NOT?

Beginning in 1967, a number of states—starting with Colorado—liberalized their abortion laws. They allowed women to have abortions under certain circumstances, such as if the pregnancy resulted from

A PROBLEM OF SOCIETY

"We are giving our time not only because we want to make abortions safer, cheaper and more accessible for the individual women who come to us, but because we see the whole abortion issue as a problem of society. . . . Women should have the right to control their own bodies and lives. Only a woman who is pregnant can determine whether she has enough resources—economic, physical and emotional—at a given time to bear and rear a child."

From the original informational pamphlet distributed by the referral service Jane, established in Chicago in 1969 to help women find safe (but illegal) abortions

Below: A pro-choice rally, in support of a woman's right to have an abortion, in 1972. The abortion issue remains controversial today.

TURNING POINT

OUR BODIES, OURSELVES

In 1969, twelve women got together in Boston, Massachusetts to talk about their bodies and their health. It was the first time many of them had discussed these topics. They realized that doctors often talked down to them, did not listen to their concerns, and did not pass on information. They decided to research health issues and share what they learned with other women. The group formed the Boston Women's Health Book Collective and published a self-help booklet called *Women and Their Bodies* in 1970. The booklet was such a success that in 1973 the group turned it into a commercial edition called *Our Bodies, Ourselves*. The bestselling book gave women straightforward information on sex, birth control, pregnancy, menopause, and other issues that enabled them to make informed decisions about their health.

Left: The cover of an early edition of *Our Bodies, Ourselves.* A number of new and revised editions of the bestselling women's health book have been published over the years.

rape or incest. Women began to discuss the topic publicly. The feminist group Redstockings held a speakout on abortion in New York City in 1969, encouraging women to discuss their experiences openly. In 1970, four states—New York, Alaska, Hawaii, and Washington—passed laws allowing a woman to have an abortion on demand, but the procedure remained controversial. In November 1972, the television show *Maude* featured a story about the forty-seven-year-old title character becoming pregnant and deciding to have an abortion. (She lived in New York, so the procedure was legal.) Thousands of viewers wrote letters of protest.

ROE V. WADE

On January 22, 1973, the Supreme Court made a landmark ruling in the case of *Roe v. Wade*, legalizing abortion throughout the United States. The Court based its decision on the belief that abortion involved a woman's constitutional right to privacy. Justice Harry Blackmun wrote the Court's decision. Years later, when he retired, he said of the decision, "It's a step that had to be taken as we go down the road toward the full emancipation of women."

The Court laid out a specific timetable for abortions. During the first three months of pregnancy, a woman could have an abortion on demand. During the second three months, states could regulate abortion but not prohibit it. During the last three months, states could prohibit abortion unless the woman's life was in danger.

Right: Scientist and writer Rachel Carson launched the modern environmental movement with her groundbreaking book, *Silent Spring*, in 1962.

BREAKTHROUGH BIOGRAPHY

RACHEL CARSON (1907–64)

Rachel Carson was a popular science writer and a marine biologist, working for the government. Almost without meaning to, she launched the modern environmental movement when she published the book *Silent Spring* in 1962. *Silent Spring* revealed that the overuse of chemical pesticides—especially DDT—had a very damaging effect on birds, fish, and humans. The chemical industry criticized Carson, but President Kennedy's Science Advisory Committee looked into the book's claims and supported them. In 1972, DDT was banned in the United States. Carson's work made the public aware of the environment and how it could be harmed. She never married, but after the deaths of her father and sister, supported her mother and two nieces. She was diagnosed with breast cancer in 1960 and ultimately died of the disease.

TURNING POINT

A NEW OPENNESS ABOUT BREAST CANCER

In 1972, Shirley Temple Black—a former child star who went on to a career in politics—went public and spoke about her experience with breast cancer and mastectomy. Black's openness about the disease came at a time when cancer was considered an issue that people did not talk about but dealt with in private. In 1974, First Lady Betty Ford also announced she had breast cancer and was having a mastectomy and chemotherapy. Ford's frankness increased public awareness of breast cancer and inspired many women to examine themselves for the disease and visit their doctors for mammograms.

Left: Betty Ford at a press conference at the White House, Washington, D.C., in 1974, around the time of her breast cancer surgery.

PRO-LIFE GROUPS

The debate on abortion continued, with people divided into "pro-choice" and "pro-life" groups. The National Right to Life Committee was established in 1973 to work against abortion, and in 1974 the first March for Life demonstration was held in Washington, D.C. The anti-abortion movement sometimes turned violent, with attacks on clinics where the procedure was performed. Steps were also taken in various states to limit or regulate abortion, such as rules that required parents or spouses to be notified or laws requiring waiting periods before an abortion could be carried out. In addition, in 1976, Congress passed the so-called Hyde Amendment, which barred federal funding for abortions for poorer women.

LESBIAN RIGHTS

Early one June morning in 1969, police raided the Stonewall Inn, a bar in New York City that was popular with gay men and lesbians. Even though gay people had become more open about their sexuality in cities such as New York and San Francisco and a small gay activist movement

Above: Women take part in a gay freedom parade in San Francisco in 1979.

had arisen, raids and other types of discrimination were common. The Stonewall raid was different, though, because this time, people fought back. Rioting went on for three days, and a new era in gay activism began. Groups such as the Gay Liberation Front formed. These groups made sexual orientation a political issue, and worked for public acceptance of homosexuality. They demanded the repeal of laws that made homosexual activity a crime, and called for new laws to ban discrimination against gays in housing and employment. Meanwhile, NOW supported lesbian rights, stating that lesbians were "doubly oppressed" since they faced injustices both as women and as homosexuals.

A number of anti-gay laws were changed in the 1970s. In 1972, East Lansing, Michigan became the first city in the United States to adopt a hiring policy that did not discriminate based on sexual orientation. In 1974, similar

WOMEN OF COURAGE AND CONVICTION

ELAINE NOBEL (1944–)

After studying at Boston University, Emerson College, and Harvard University, Elaine Nobel worked as a speech instructor. She also became active in Boston's gay community. In 1974, Nobel became the first openly gay person to be elected to public office when she successfully ran for a seat in the Massachusetts state legislature. She described the campaign as "ugly." Gunshots were fired, windows were broken at her campaign headquarters, and people visiting her were threatened. Nobel was elected to a second term in 1976, this time with almost 90 percent of the vote. After serving two terms, she worked for the mayor of Boston. She unsuccessfully ran for office a number of times, then worked in health care. Nobel later retired and moved to Florida.

antidiscrimination laws were passed in Columbus, Ohio; Alfred, New York; and St. Paul, Minnesota. Other cities followed.

VIOLENCE AGAINST WOMEN

Largely as a result of the women's movement, the public became aware of domestic violence—the physical and/or mental abuse inflicted upon someone by his or her spouse or partner. Feminists charged that the criminal justice system did not take violence against women seriously or hold men accountable for it. Shelters began to be set up so that female victims of domestic abuse had a place to go. By 1979, there were more than 250 such shelters in the United States. Women also began to be provided with services such as counseling and legal aid. The National Coalition Against Domestic Violence was founded in 1978.

RECLAIMING THE NIGHT

Women also took to the streets to protest violence against women, including rape. The first such march for women in the United States took place in 1976. The following year, women began using the phrase "Take back the night" to describe their efforts to make the streets safe for women going out in the evenings.

TURNING POINT

CHANGING ATTITUDES TOWARD RAPE

Susan Brownmiller's landmark book *Against Our Will: Men, Women and Rape* was published in 1975. It did much to change public attitudes about rape. Before the book appeared, many people saw rape as the victim's fault. They felt that women teased men, dressed suggestively, or acted in other unwise ways. Brownmiller and other feminists held that rape was about power, not sex. After *Against Our Will* came out, many state rape laws were changed so that, for example, women no longer needed to have three witnesses to the incident. States also began to pass laws saying that husbands could be charged with raping their wives.

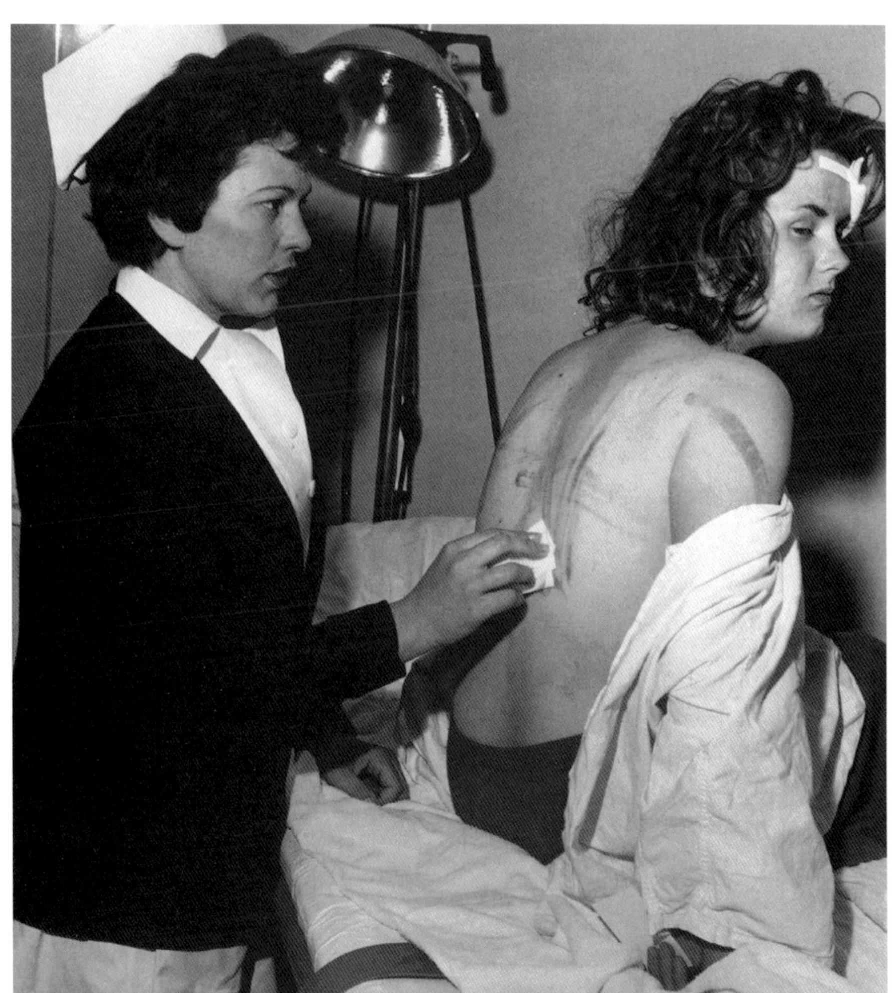

Left: A nurse treats the wounds on a young woman's back, the result of a beating by her husband. The women's movement made the public aware of the problem of domestic violence.

CHAPTER 7

Arts and Culture

The feminist movement inspired many women to create new works of art, literature, and music that reflected their changing lives. To some extent, popular culture—such as television programs, movies, and bestsellers—did not always reflect the more serious works that were created. Yet women artists, writers, and musicians found new audiences and recognition for the thoughtful, significant works they created, many of which are still admired today.

TURNING POINT

TWO IMPORTANT NOVELS

The year 1973 saw the publication of two sensational books. Erica Jong's *Fear of Flying* was a witty, graphic depiction of a woman's pursuit of sexual experiences and personal and professional fulfillment. Jong was one of the first popular female authors to explore female sexuality without shame and with great humor. She later said, "I wanted to create a thinking woman who also had a sexual life." Rita Mae Brown's *Rubyfruit Jungle* was similarly adventurous, but her book focused on an outrageous, outspoken lesbian. The book became a hit with both feminist and gay readers.

NOVELISTS

From colonial times, American women had written to express their feelings and tell about their experiences. With the feminist movement of the 1960s and 1970s, women found new opportunities to exercise their creativity. They also began to focus increasingly on such issues as race, sexuality, and personal freedoms.

Author Toni Morrison often explored African-American heritage and history, and produced a string of notable books, beginning with her

Right: A scene from the 1979 television movie *I Know Why the Caged Bird Sings*, based on the book by Maya Angelou.

first novel, *The Bluest Eye* (1970). It told of a young black girl who is convinced she is ugly and wishes she had blue eyes. Morrison continued her success with *Sula* (1973), about the intertwined lives of two black women, and *Song of Solomon* (1977). The latter combined such elements as fantasy, fable, and song as the main character celebrates his African-American heritage to discover his true self.

Another African-American writer, Maya Angelou, wrote the powerful *I Know Why the Caged Bird Sings* in 1970. It told of the traumas she experienced growing up poor and black during the Depression. African-American women particularly embraced Angelou's works, which include poetry, plays, and screenplays.

CHINESE-AMERICAN AUTHORS

Among Asian-American writers, Maxine Hong Kingston—the daughter of Chinese immigrants—said there were no books about Chinese Americans when she was growing up. In 1976 she wrote *The Woman Warrior: Memoirs of a Girlhood Among Ghosts*, a fantastic tale blending legends, history, and stories her mother had told her. Bette Bao Lord,

TURNING POINT

THE *LADIES HOME JOURNAL* SIT-IN

Millions of women in the 1960s and 1970s read the *Ladies Home Journal*, which featured articles on cooking, stories about romance, and other pieces that highlighted women's traditional roles. In March 1970, more than one hundred women from groups such as NOW and Redstockings staged a sit-in in the office of John Mack Carter, the magazine's editor and publisher. They were protesting the image of women portrayed by the magazine, and the fact that women were not in charge of the publication. They demanded that the magazine provide free day care for employees, stop accepting ads that degraded women, and change its editorial focus to support the goals of the feminist movement. After eleven hours, Carter agreed to publish a special section of the magazine on women's legal rights and status. Several years later, a woman was named editor of the magazine for the first time.

Left: Maxine Hong Kingston, whose books blend elements of myth, legend, and history with autobiography.

Above: A scene from Ntozake Shange's *for colored girls who have considered suicide/when the rainbow is enuf*, which was produced on Broadway in 1976.

BREAKTHROUGH BIOGRAPHY

SYLVIA PLATH (1932–63)

Sylvia Plath's first poem was published in *Seventeen* magazine in 1950, before she entered Smith College on a scholarship. In 1953, Plath suffered a breakdown and attempted suicide. After graduating from Smith in 1955, she studied at Cambridge University in England. She married the English poet Ted Hughes in 1956. Meanwhile, Plath published her first volume of poetry, *The Colossus*, in 1960. Her best-known work, *The Bell Jar*—a novel about her emotional breakdown—appeared in England in 1963. (It was not published in the United States until 1971.) Plath took her own life in February 1963, leaving behind a series of powerful, angry poems that were published after her death in the volume *Ariel*. Feminists hailed Plath's work as a groundbreaking example of confessional poetry concerning the female condition and helped turn her into a cult figure.

who was born in Shanghai, China, and moved to the United States as a child, published her first book in 1964. *Eighth Moon: The True Story of a Young Girl's Life in Communist China* told of the separation of Lord's sister from her family when she was unable to travel with them to the United States.

POETS AND POETRY

The poet Audre Lorde wrote from her perspective as an African American, a woman, and a lesbian. Her first book of poetry, *The First Cities,* appeared in 1968. She published several other volumes of poetry during the 1970s, including *From a Land Where Other People Live* (1973). Another celebrated feminist poet was Adrienne Rich, whose powerful works demanded justice for the unfair treatment given to women, the poor, and other groups. Her collection *Diving into the Wreck* (1973) won a National Book Award. Nikki

Giovanni, whose poems addressed her development as a militant black activist, was extremely popular and was named Woman of the Year by the *Ladies Home Journal* in 1972.

PLAYS AND PLAYWRIGHTS

Women also produced works for the stage. Ntozake Shange's *for colored girls who have considered suicide/when the rainbow is enuf* appeared on Broadway in New York City in 1976. A set of twenty choreographed poems and vignettes, it marked the first time since 1959 that a play by an African-American woman had been produced on Broadway. Marsha Norman (who would go on to win a Pulitzer Prize for drama in 1983 for *'night, Mother*) had her first plays produced in the 1970s, including *Getting Out* and *Third and Oak*. Wendy Wasserstein (who also won a Pulitzer Prize in 1989 for *The Heidi Chronicles*) had her first major success with *Uncommon Women and Others* (1978). It told about eight female college students making decisions about their lives at the height of the women's movement in the early 1970s.

TURNING POINT

FREE TO BE . . . YOU AND ME

In 1972, actress Marlo Thomas and a group of her celebrity friends released a children's record album called *Free to Be . . . You and Me*. The record promoted individuality and tolerance, with the major theme that anyone—boy or girl—could achieve anything he or she wanted. Among the songs were "It's All Right to Cry" (sung by a former professional football player) and "William's Doll" (about a boy who wants to practice being a good father). A *Free to Be* book appeared in 1973, and a TV special followed the next year. Thomas created *Free to Be* when she could not find nonsexist books for her young niece. "I was shocked to find that all the children's books I found reinforced old gender stereotypes of what girls and boys were supposed to be or ought to be," Thomas said. "None of them talked about all the possibilities of what girls and boys *could* be."

Left: Actress Marlo Thomas organized a group of celebrities to produce *Free to Be . . . You and Me*, which challenged gender stereotypes.

> **LOOK HOW MUCH I GAINED...**
>
> *"I am woman, hear me roar*
> *In numbers too big to ignore*
> *And I know too much to go back and pretend*
> *'Cause I've heard it all before*
> *And I've been down there on the floor*
> *No one's ever gonna keep me down again*
> *Oh, yes, I am wise*
> *But it's wisdom born of pain*
> *Yes, I paid the price*
> *But look how much I gained.*
> *If I have to, I can do anything*
> *I am strong*
> *I am invincible*
> *I am woman."*
>
> From Helen Reddy's song "I Am Woman" (1972), which became the unofficial anthem of the feminist movement

POPULAR MUSIC

Women made their mark in different types of music. The "girl groups" that first became popular in the late 1950s had a lasting influence. The groups were made up of several young women who sang emotionally about their problems and the search for love, often involving a boy who was misunderstood. Some girl groups were white—such as the Angels (who had a hit record with "My Boyfriend's Back") and the Shangri Las (who sang "Leader of the Pack")—but most were black.

Among the top black groups were the Marvelettes ("Please Mr. Postman") and Martha Reeves and the Vandellas ("Heat

Right: Girl group the Supremes, led by Diana Ross (right), had twelve number-one singles during the 1960s.

Wave"). The Supremes were by far the most successful group. Their first number one song—"Where Did Our Love Go?"—was released in 1964. Numerous hits followed, including "Baby Love" and "Someday We'll Be Together." Fronted by lead singer Diana Ross, the Supremes wore glamorous gowns and became international stars, frequently appearing on television.

SOUL AND FOLK SINGERS

Another African-American performer who stood out from the crowd was Aretha Franklin, who sang soul and rhythm and blues (R&B). Franklin—who came to be known as the Queen of Soul—had her first hit in 1967 with "I Never Loved a Man (The Way I Love You)." Her

BREAKTHROUGH BIOGRAPHY

JANIS JOPLIN (1943–70)

While she was growing up Janis Joplin was drawn to classic blues music, and rebelled against accepted standards of femininity. In 1966, Joplin joined Big Brother and the Holding Company, a hard rock band in San Francisco, California. She became a superstar, a larger-than-life figure who performed with wild abandon as she sang in a commanding, raspy blues voice. Big Brother's second album, *Cheap Thrills* (1968), featured one of her best-known songs, "Piece of My Heart," and sold a million copies. However, Joplin developed a serious dependency on drugs and alcohol, and left the band. In August 1969 she performed at Woodstock, the three-day music festival in Bethel, New York, attended by hundreds of thousands of young people. In October 1970, while working on the album *Pearl* in Los Angeles, she died from an accidental overdose of heroin. She is still viewed by many people as one of rock music's greatest performers.

Left: Although Janis Joplin was already suffering from the effects of her drug addiction when she appeared at Woodstock in 1969, she still gave a powerful performance.

signature song was "Respect." In it, she demanded that her worth and dignity be recognized. Both the civil rights movement and the women's movement adopted the song as one of their anthems.

Meanwhile, folk music showed the rebellious nature of the times since many of its star acts—such as Joan Baez—were political activists. Baez brought attention to causes such as civil rights and opposition to the Vietnam War, and she was arrested a number of times for her activities. Odetta—who sang at the 1963 civil rights March on Washington—was one of the few African Americans popular with the mostly white folk audience.

ROCK

In the area of rock music, Carole King began her career writing some of the songs recorded by girl groups. She then started recording her own songs, and her 1971 album *Tapestry* became one of the top-selling records of all time. Grace Slick joined the psychedelic band Jefferson Airplane in 1966. As the group's lead singer, she became one of the most famous women in rock, her voice driving the songs "Somebody to Love" and "White Rabbit." A true trailblazer was

WOMEN OF COURAGE AND CONVICTION

LINDA NOCHLIN (1931–)

Linda Nochlin studied at Vassar College and Columbia University and received her doctoral degree from New York University's Institute of Fine Arts in 1963. She taught art history at many universities. In 1971 she wrote an essay in *Art News* magazine called "Why Have There Been No Great Women Artists?" It was a landmark paper that sparked a flurry of feminist writings. In the essay, Nochlin discussed the social structures that influenced women's art and examined why their works had not been given the same status as men's. In 1976, Nochlin and another professor, Ann Sutherland Harris, organized an important exhibit called "Women Artists, 1550–1950" that traveled to different museums. The exhibit included many women artists whose work had long been ignored.

Right: Singer and songwriter Patti Smith, who came to fame in the 1970s, was inducted into the Rock and Roll Hall of Fame in 2007.

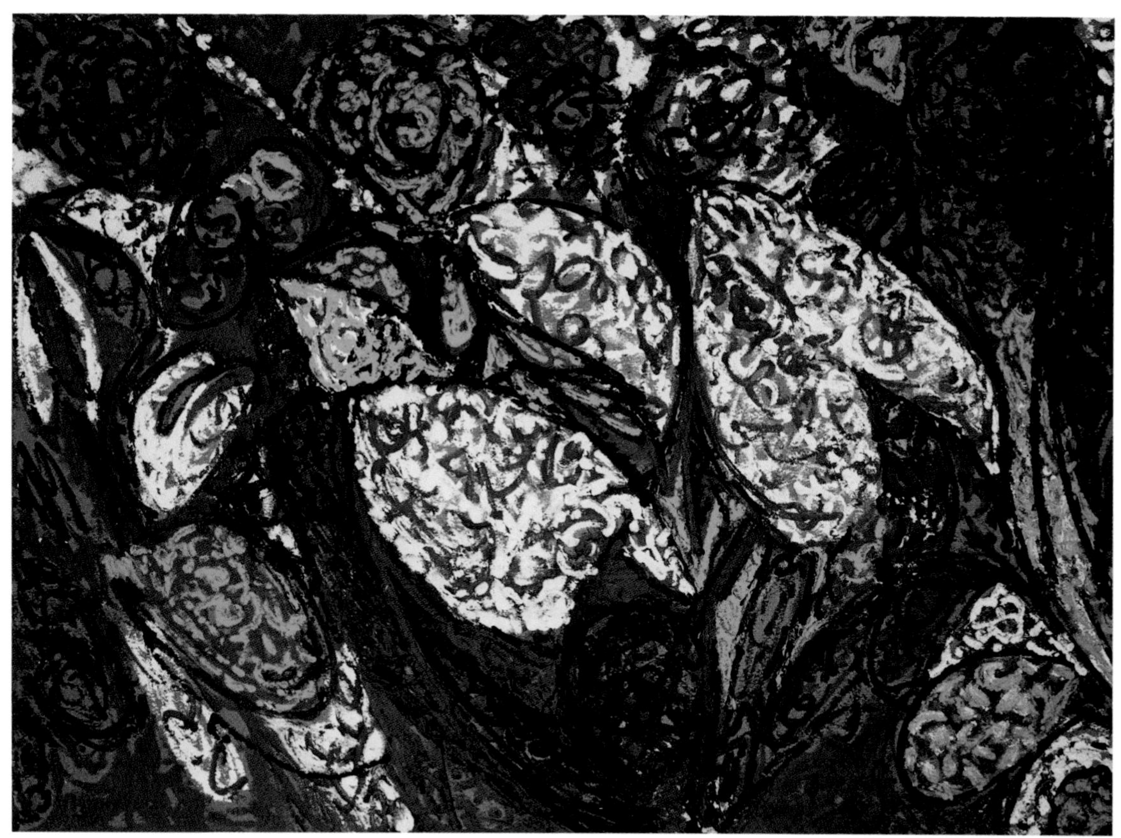

Left: A 1965 painting by Lee Krasner (1908–84), an abstract expressionist painter whose works influenced many artists.

Patti Smith, who is seen as the mother of alternative rock music. Smith recorded her first album, *Horses*, in 1975. In her unconventional stage act, she presented a sullen figure, reciting poetry and singing in a gritty voice. Smith achieved popularity with the mainstream and was a huge influence on future rock musicians.

VISUAL ARTS

Before the 1960s, women artists struggled to find a place in exhibitions and were under-represented in scholarly studies of the history of art. Feminist art historians insisted that works by women artists be included in both.

Museums began to acknowledge the important contributions made by women. In 1972, the Guggenheim Museum in New York City mounted its first major show devoted to a woman—the sculptor and painter Eva Hesse, who died in 1970. In addition, many contemporary women artists made their mark, including Alice Neel, Lee Krasner, Nancy Spero, Joyce Wieland, and Cindy Sherman. Still, women had relatively few places to exhibit their art. In response, in 1972, a group of women artists in New York founded A.I.R. (Artists in Residence)—the first cooperative gallery for women artists in the United States.

TURNING POINT

"THE DINNER PARTY" OPENS

In 1979, artist Judy Chicago presented "The Dinner Party," a huge installation celebrating the achievements of 999 real and mythical women throughout history. The project was made up of a large triangular table with individual place settings honoring famous women, including feminist Susan B. Anthony, writer Virginia Woolf, and artist Georgia O'Keeffe. The tile "Heritage Floor" beneath the table had the names of hundreds of other women written in gold. Chicago designed the entire project, but she created it with the help of hundreds of mostly female volunteer craftspeople.

CHAPTER 8

THE PERIOD IN BRIEF

COMPARED WITH THE PRESENT DAY, LIFE FOR WOMEN was very different in 1960. Back then, most women's ambitions were confined to marriage, home and family. Today women have numerous choices about their personal and professional lives that were previously not available to them. In large part, they won the freedom to make those choices during the years 1961 to 1979.

> **HERE I AM**
>
> *"It was 144 years ago that members of the Democratic Party first met in convention to select a presidential candidate. Since that time, Democrats have continued to convene once every four years. . . . But there is something different about tonight. . . . What is different? What is special? I, Barbara Jordan, am a keynote speaker. A lot of years passed since 1832, and during that time it would have been most unusual for any national political party to ask that a Barbara Jordan deliver a keynote address. But tonight here I am."*
>
> Representative Barbara Jordan, an African-American woman, delivering the keynote address at the 1976 Democratic convention

MOVES TOWARD EQUALITY

The women's movement brought tremendous change to the United States. As a result of new laws, lawsuits, and court decisions—and the actions of many brave people—the nation became a different place, and women made great strides toward equality. There were laws saying they could no longer be discriminated against in the world of work. Schools and colleges had to provide equal funding for women's programs—which was especially evident in the area of sports. Banks and finance

Right: By 1979, more women had joined the workforce in jobs traditionally held by men. These women are employed as members of an air-force crew.

companies could no longer refuse to give loans, credit cards, or mortgages to unmarried women. And they could not require wives to get their husbands' signatures on the papers.

THE WORLD OPENS UP

Things were not perfect. Companies and organizations did not always follow the law. Discrimination against women still existed. But the world had opened up for many women—and for the first time, they had choices. They could go to college and then on to architecture, medical, dental, or law school. They could apply for jobs as engineers, airline pilots, police officers, judges, or plumbers. They could get married or stay single. They could have children when young, or choose to wait until their careers were established before having children, or not have any at all. If they preferred, they could still follow the traditional route and become a wife, mother, and homemaker. The important thing was that for the first time, women could decide.

Women now had the courage to stand up for what they wanted. They could tell their husbands to help with the housework, ask their bosses for a raise, and end personal relationships that were harmful or unfulfilling. Those important freedoms had not existed before the women's movement of the 1960s and 1970s.

TURNING POINT

THE MARY TYLER MOORE SHOW

The Mary Tyler Moore Show had its debut on television in September 1970. The main character, Mary Richards, was a career-oriented single woman in her thirties who had just broken up with her boyfriend. Determined to make it on her own, she moves to Minneapolis, Minnesota, and gets a job at a TV station. The show was one of the first to portray a woman who was happy at her job and content to be single. By the time the show went off the air in 1977, it had become one of the most popular situation comedies ever, and its heroine had become a symbol for a generation of a woman who did not need a husband or children to make her happy.

Left: The central character on *The Mary Tyler Moore Show*—an unmarried career woman—was very different from any that had ever been shown on TV.

Timeline

1961	January 20: John F. Kennedy is inaugurated as president. The President's Commission on the Status of Women is created to investigate the condition of women in the United States.
1962	September: Rachel Carson's book *Silent Spring* marks the start of the modern environmental movement.
1963	Betty Friedan's *The Feminine Mystique* is published. June: The Equal Pay Act is passed, prohibiting salary discrimination based on sex. October 11: The President's Commission on the Status of Women issues its report, finding widespread discrimination against women. November 22: President Kennedy is shot and killed in Dallas, Texas; Lyndon Johnson is sworn in as president.
1964	July 2: the Civil Rights Act is signed into law, prohibiting discrimination on the basis of race, color, religion, sex, or national origin; the Equal Employment Opportunity Commission (EEOC) is created to investigate complaints. At the Republican National Convention, Senator Margaret Chase Smith becomes the first woman nominated for president by a major political party.
1965	August 6: The Voting Rights Act is signed into law.
1966	The National Organization for Women (NOW) is founded, with Betty Friedan as its first president.
1967	Activist groups such as the New York Radical Women and the Chicago Women's Liberation Group are founded. April 19: Kathy Switzer enters the Boston Maraton as "K. Switzer" and finishes the race, despite the efforts of an event official to stop her.
1968	August 5: The EEOC rules that help wanted ads can no longer be divided into "male" and "female" categories. September: The New York Radical Women stage a protest at the Miss America Pageant in New Jersey, tossing items like bras and girdles into a "Freedom Trash Can." November: Shirley Chisholm becomes the first African-American woman elected to Congress.
1969	June 28: Riots break out following a raid by New York City police on the Stonewall Inn, launching the gay and lesbian rights movement. August: Hundreds of thousands of young people gather at the Woodstock music festival near Bethel, New York. September 5: California's "no-fault" divorce act is signed into law.
1970	August 26: More than 100,000 women hold rallies during the Women's Strike for Equality. San Diego State University offers the nation's first official women's studies program.
1971	The National Women's Political Caucus is founded to encourage women to run for office.

1972	January: *Ms.* magazine begins publication with its "preview" issue. March 22: Congress passes the Equal Rights Amendment and sends it to the states for ratification; soon after, Phyllis Schlafly launches STOP ERA to prevent ratification. June 23: Title IX of the Education Amendments of 1972 prohibits sex discrimination in educational institutions receiving federal funds, opening up school sports to women and girls.
1973	January 22: The Supreme Court legalizes abortion in the case of *Roe v. Wade.* September 20: Billie Jean King defeats Bobby Riggs in the tennis "Battle of the Sexes." *Our Bodies, Ourselves* is published, providing straightforward information on women's health.
1974	The first antiabortion "March for Life" takes place in Washington, D.C.
1975	January 21: The Supreme Court rules that it is unconstitutional to exclude women from serving on juries.
1976	Women enter the nation's military service academies for the first time. September: Congress passes the Hyde Amendment, eliminating federal funding for abortions for poorer women.
1977	November 18–21: The National Women's Conference is held in Houston, Texas, to evaluate the status of women and decide on future goals.
1978	More women than men enter college for the first time. October: the Pregnancy Discrimination Act bans employment discrimination against pregnant women. Congress votes to extend the deadline for ratification of the ERA, from 1979 to 1982. In 2010, the ERA required ratification by three out of the necessary thirty-eight states, which meant it was still not part of the U.S. Constitution.

GLOSSARY AND FURTHER INFORMATION

abortion A procedure to terminate a pregnancy.

activists People who take action in support of or in opposition to an issue.

affirmative action Programs set up to improve the opportunities of minorities and women to make up for past discrimination.

boycotts Actions in which people refuse to deal with a business or other organization because they oppose its policies.

caucus A group of people who get together to promote a particular policy or certain interests.

chauffeured When someone is driven by car from place to place.

chemotherapy A treatment for cancer and other conditions involving the use of chemical agents.

civil rights The basic rights that every person should have, such as voting, education, choice of religion, freedom of movement, and ownership of property.

comfort zones Physical and/or psychological circumstances in which people feel most at ease and free from distress.

contraceptive A birth-control device, used to prevent pregnancy.

convenience foods Ready meals that have been made commercially, so need little preparation by the consumer.

counterculture A culture that has ideas, values, and ways of behaving that differ from those of the larger society. Beatniks and hippies of the 1960s were examples of countercultural movements.

DDT An insecticide, banned in many countries since the 1970s, that is dangerous to people and animals.

denominations Groupings within a religious faith.

diversity A variety—sometimes refers to having different genders and ethnic and socioeconomic groups represented in an organization or society.

feminism A movement to gain opportunities and rights for women that are equal to those of men.

hormones Chemicals made by certain glands in the body; also refers to synthetic chemicals that are used in medical treatment.

juries Panels of people who decide whether a person accused of a crime is guilty or innocent during a trial.

labor unions Organizations that act for better working conditions for their members.

lesbian A woman who is sexually attracted to other women.

mainstream Ideas, values, and actions that are most widely accepted by a group or society.

mammogram An X-ray taken of the breast to detect disease.

mastectomy A surgical treatment for breast cancer in which the breast is removed.

menopause The time in a woman's life, generally between the ages of forty-five and fifty, when she stops menstruating.

migrant A person who moves around from place to place to do seasonal work.

nuclear weapons Explosive weapons that use the power created by splitting atoms.

oppressed Treated in an unjust, cruel way.

ordained Officially appointed as a priest, minister, or rabbi.

pesticides Chemicals used to kill insects.

picket line A organized group of people, usually outside a building, protesting something; picket lines are often made up of striking workers.

potential What a person is capable of achieving in the future.

psychedelic Involving drugs that cause hallucinations or altered mental states, or the wild, colorful images or sounds experienced by someone under the influence of such drugs.

radical A person or position that favors extreme change.

rape The crime of forcing a person to have sex.

segregation The separation of people of different races.

service industries Industries that provide services for people rather than producing goods for sale.

sexual revolution A relaxation in standards of sexual behavior such as occurred in the 1960s in the United States.

sharecroppers People who farm land that is owned by someone else.

suburban Relating to the suburbs—areas on the outskirts of cities.

suffragists People in the late 1800s and early 1900s who campaigned for the right to vote.

tenure A position, especially at a college or university, that is secure and permanent until retirement.

BOOKS

Collins, Gail. *When Everything Changed: The Amazing Journey of American Women From 1960 to the Present.* New York: Little, Brown and Company, 2009.

Fisanick, Christina, editor. *Feminism.* Detroit, Michigan: Greenhaven Press, 2007.

Friedman, Lauri S., editor. *Women's Rights.* Detroit, Michigan: Greenhaven Press, 2010.

Gourley, Catherine. *Gidgets and Women Warriors: Perceptions of Women in the 1950s and 1960s.* Minneapolis, Minnesota: Twenty-First Century Books, 2008.

Gourley, Catherine. *Ms. and the Material Girl: Perceptions of Women from the 1970s Through the 1990s.* Minneapolis, Minnesota: Twenty-First Century Books, 2008.

Kallen, Stuart A. *Women of the Civil Rights Movement.* San Diego, California: Lucent Books, 2005.

Schomp, Virginia. *American Voices from the Women's Movement.* Tarrytown, New York: Marshall Cavendish Benchmark, 2007.

WEB SITES

http://www.feminist.org/research/chronicles/chronicl.html

http://www.justicelearning.org/ViewIssue.aspx?IssueID=13

http://www.legacy98.org/index.html

http://www.pbs.org/wgbh/amex/pill/index.html

http://www.titleix.info/

DVDs

Equality: History of the Women's Movement in America (Schlessinger Video, 1995)

Step by Step: Building a Feminist Movement, 1941–1977 (Women Make Movies, 1998)

Index

Numbers in **bold** refer to illustrations.